BUILDING A CORE PRINT
COLLECTION FOR PRESCHOOLERS

ALA Editions purchases fund advocacy, awareness,
and accreditation programs for library professionals worldwide.

Building a Core Print Collection for Preschoolers

ALAN R. BAILEY

An imprint of the American Library Association

Chicago   2014

Over his thirty-year career as a professional librarian, **Alan R. Bailey** has served as a public school librarian and as a branch manager of a public library, and he has worked in community college and university libraries. For more than eighteen of those years, he has been directly responsible for developing collections for young children. A native of Washington, North Carolina, Bailey received his under-graduate degree from East Carolina University (Greenville, NC) and advanced degrees from East Carolina University and North Carolina Central University (Durham, NC). Alan currently serves as associate professor and education cur-riculum librarian in the Teaching Resources Center at East Carolina University's J. Y. Joyner Library. Bailey has served multiple terms as a member of the Coretta Scott King Book Awards Jury and has reviewed books for the "Children's Litera-ture Review" column in *Language Arts: The Journal of the Elementary Section of the National Council of Teachers of English.*

© 2014 by the American Library Association

Printed in the United States of America

18 17 16 15 14   5 4 3 2 1

ISBNs: 978-0-8389-1219-5 (paper); 978-0-8389-1978-1 (PDF); 978-0-8389-1979-8 (ePub); 978-0-8389-1980-4 (Kindle). For more information on digital formats, visit the ALA Store at alastore.ala.org and select eEditions.

Library of Congress Cataloging-in-Publication Data
Bailey, Alan R.
 Building a core print collection for preschoolers / Alan R. Bailey.
  pages cm
 Includes bibliographical references and index.
  ISBN 978-0-8389-1219-5 (print : alk. paper)—ISBN 978-0-8389-1978-1 (pdf)—ISBN 978-0-8389-1979-8 (epub)—ISBN 978-0-8389-1980-4 (kindle) 1. Children's libraries—United States—Book lists. 2. Preschool children—Books and reading—United States. 3. Libraries and preschool children—United States. I. Title.
 Z718.2.U6B35 2014
 027.62'5--dc23

                                2014001000

Cover design by Chelsea Cook. Image © Monkey Business Images; Shutterstock, Inc.
Text design by Mayfly Design in the Whitman and ITC Officina Sans Std typefaces

∞ This paper meets the requirements of ANSI/NISO Z39.48–1992 (Permanence of Paper).

Contents

Preface

What Is a Core Collection?

The titles selected and annotated in this book are examples of the most essential books for children from birth to age five. This noteworthy core collection, containing adeptly chosen books for preschoolers and representing a broad span of interests, backgrounds, abilities, and cultural experiences, enhances literacy skills, establishes and improves reading skills, and provides many learning advantages. These learning advantages include expressive and receptive language, expanded vocabularies, narrative skills, print awareness, the ability to understand written language, awareness of story structure, alphabetic knowledge, and phonological sensitivity.

Although this is a definitive list of core materials, it is not all-inclusive. Considering the multitude of materials published for children annually, readers are sure to find one or more of their personal favorites missing from this book. Readers will find, however, more than three hundred annotated citations that a broad range of children from birth to age five will find memorable and pleasurable while also having their intellectual, developmental, cultural, language, cognitive, creative, communication, and social needs met.

Why Is This Book Relevant?

Reading aloud clearly affects kindergarten readiness and lifelong literacy; therefore, reading to children is one of the most important things that educators, parents, and child-care professionals can do for a child. Years prior to entering school, a child's foundation for learning and experiencing formal reading instruction is in place, and reading to children daily enhances that foundation. Early exposure to books heavily influences vocabulary knowledge, which in turn improves reading skills and lifelong literacy. Primary skills books, nursery rhymes, wordless picture books, toy and movable books, rhyming books, fingerplays and action rhymes, and board books not only are entertaining and enjoyable to preschoolers but also are designed to meet their intellectual, developmental, cultural, language, cognitive, creative, communication, and social needs as well. Titles annotated in this book, in conjunction with the accompanying recommended resources, provide educators, child-care professionals, and parents with resources that are instrumental in providing preschool children the literacy foundations needed to succeed from kindergarten through their adult lives.

There is a critical need for a reference tool to assist librarians, professors, early childhood educators, parents, and other child-care providers of children from birth to kindergarten as they build recommended reading lists and core collections. *Building a Core Print Collection for Preschoolers* is that resource. In addition to being timely and essential, it is the only book devoted exclusively to creating a core collection for children in this age range.

Who Is the Audience for This Book?

The primary audience for *Building a Core Print Collection for Preschoolers* is practicing librarians. However, early childhood professionals, preservice teachers and librarians, parents, professors, and other child-care providers of preschool children will find this work equally significant. This unique book is a valued addition to every public library, elementary school library, and college and university library with early childhood education programs. It is a welcome addition to professional collections of both child-care centers and churches with vigorous youth programs, and it can serve as a required or recommended text for literature, reading, and early childhood classes on college and university campuses. In essence, *Building a Core Print Collection for Preschoolers* is the starting point for anyone establishing a preschool collection and an essential resource to individuals committed to expanding or enhancing an existing collection.

Which Criteria Were Used?

Reviews in professional journals; recommendations from librarians, parents, teachers, children, and other individuals involved in children's literature; recommended reading lists; and many of the author's favorite children's books provided the initial titles for the book. After I read each title, I considered a series of questions. I selected only those titles that received an overwhelming number of affirmative replies to the following questions:

- Is the language clear and appropriate for children from birth to age five?
- Are the illustrations clear and appropriate for children from birth to age five?
- Does the complexity and development of the book match the child's developmental stage?
- Is the text accurate?
- Is the story clear?
- Is the writing style consistent?
- Does the book read aloud well?
- Do the words and illustrations complement each other?
- Do the illustrations primarily tell the story?
- Does the story flow?
- Will children be drawn to the book?
- Does the book avoid gender, racial, and other stereotypes?
- Overall, is the layout of the book, including font, colors, size, and so on, impressive?

Out-of-Print Titles

Unfortunately, several core titles listed in this book are no longer in print. For those titles, both new and gently used copies are available via Amazon .com and BookFinder.com. Both companies sell millions of used books, and you are likely to find the book you desire at a reasonable price.

Review Sources

In addition to annotations, review sources from nine highly recognized children's resources are included. These sources include *Booklist*, *Children's Literature* (accessible through *Children's Literature Comprehensive Database*), *Horn Book Guide to Children's and Young Adult Books*, *Horn Book Magazine*, *Kirkus Reviews*, *Library Journal*, *Publisher's Weekly*, *School Library Journal*, and *Wilson Library Bulletin* (ceased in 1995). Additional information relating to these and other review sources can be found in the "Recommended Resources for Building a Core Collection" section of this book.

Acknowledgments

This book would not have been possible without the support of so many people.

I would like to thank my parents, Harmon and Ophelia Bailey, and my five siblings, Ethel, Harmon Jr., Clifton, Wilfred, and Soisette—you have supported my educational and professional endeavors from the very beginning, and for this I am forever grateful.

A huge thank-you to the late Ms. Bobby M. Grimes, my unconventional seventh-grade homeroom and language arts teacher, for recognizing greatness in an animated young boy who was unable to envision greatness within himself. I thank you for nurturing me, convincing me that I did have what it takes to earn a college degree, and holding me accountable to standards higher than those set for most of my fellow classmates. I am sure you are teaching children how to diagram sentences in heaven . . . .

This book would not have been possible without Charles Harmon, Kathy Buchsbaum, Stephanie Zvirin, and Katherine Faydash. Charles, I sincerely thank you for believing in me and giving me a chance to transform a concept into a manuscript. Kathy, Stephanie, and Katherine, a new author could not have asked for better editors—your patience, firmness, and "gentle nudges" were reassuring throughout the process.

And finally, I would like to thank my family, friends, the team at Joyner Library's Teaching Resources Center, and members of the Unitarian Universalist Congregation of Greenville for your love, patience, and encouragement. When I asked you for thoughts and prayers of creativity and endurance, you sent them to me. I know this because the manuscript has been published.

Reading Aloud

Kindergarten Readiness and Lifelong Literacy for Preschool Children

Children develop the critical language and early-reading skills necessary to enter kindergarten between birth and age five; therefore, reading to infants is essential in boosting brain development and school readiness. In addition to being one of the ways to help a child learn, reading aloud is one of the most influential steps librarians, parents, teachers, and child-care providers can take to foster a child's literacy skills. According to a study by Nigel Hall (1987), children who cannot read in first grade remain unable to read in the fourth grade. Even more alarming, Brassell (2006) found that children who are not good readers earn less money and are not as healthy throughout life as good readers are. Reading abilities improve when children are read to and exposed to books at an early age, and this clearly affects their kindergarten readiness and lifelong learning.

Laying the Groundwork for School Readiness and Lifelong Literacy

Reading aloud to children during infancy and early adolescence provides numerous learning advantages that are essential to school readiness. Principal benefits include expressive and receptive language, expanded vocabularies, narrative skills, print awareness, the ability to understand written language, awareness of story structure, alphabetic knowledge, and phonological sensitivity. Reading aloud also encourages enthusiasm for literacy, which develops lifetime reading habits—habits crucial to lifelong literacy.

Even the youngest child enjoys being read to. Listening to adults talk is a child's initial exposure to vocabulary, which ultimately leads to a love for language. Parents and child-care providers can stimulate this love for language by reading aloud to children frequently. In addition to reading to preschoolers often, adults should demonstrate how much they value and enjoy reading by modeling reading behavior. Children need to see influential individuals engage in reading. In the years prior to entering school, a child's foundation for learning and experiencing formal reading instruction is put into place. Reading to children daily enhances that foundation and lays the essential groundwork for school readiness and lifelong literacy success.

Providing Access to Books

Access to books is crucial to language development; therefore, frequently visiting libraries and creating a home library are additional approaches to affecting a child's language, learning, and literacy skills (Brassell 2006). Books expose children to crucial school-readiness requirements, including reading and language skills, at an early age. Well-stocked home libraries not only signify the importance of reading but also craft a solid foundation for nurturing the habit of reading (Sanacore 2006). Reading aloud should provide memorable and pleasurable experiences for children and should include a variety of books to meet their intellectual, developmental, cultural, language, cognitive, creative, communication, and social interests.

Picture Books and Children Age Birth to Five

To fully support the critical developmental and literacy needs of children from birth to age five, strong library collections must be developed and sustained. Picture books, or books primarily consisting of detailed illustrations and limited text, are essential elements to such collections. The rich illustrations featured on the pages of this genre of books are as important as, if not more important than, the text in conveying the story. Primary skills books, wordless picture books, board books, toy and movable books, rhyming books, fingerplays and action rhymes, and nursery rhymes all represent the rudiments of a core collection for children ages birth to five.

Titles cited and annotated in this book, in conjunction with the accompanying recommended resources, provide librarians, parents, teachers, and child-care providers with books essential to developing and sustaining a superior preschool print collection.[1]

Note

1. Parts of this introduction were first published in *Children & Libraries: The Journal of the Association for Library Service to Children* 7, no. 3 (2009): 17–24.

References

Brassell, Danny. 2006. *Readers for Life: The Ultimate Reading Fitness Guide, K–8*. Portsmouth, NH: Heinemann.

Hall, Nigel. 1987. *The Emergence of Literacy*. Portsmouth, NH: Heinemann.

Sanacore, Joseph. 2006. "Nurturing Lifetime Readers." *Childhood Education* 83: 33–37.

Additional Sources

Arnold, Renea. 2003. "Public Libraries and Early Literacy: Raising a Reader." *American Libraries* 34: 48–51.

Bailey, Alan R. 2009. "Early Essentials: Developing and Sustaining Birth–Kindergarten Library Collections." *Children & Libraries: The Journal of the Association for Library Service to Children* 7: 17–24.

Feinberg, Sandra, Barbara Jordan, Kathleen Deerr, Marcellina Byrne, and Lisa G. Kropp. 2007. *The Family-Centered Library Handbook*. New York: Neal-Schuman Publishers.

Galda, Lee, and Bernice E. Cullinan. 2006. *Literature and the Child*. Belmont, CA: Wadsworth/Thomson Learning.

Gambrell, Linda B., Lesley Mandel Morrow, and Michael Pressley, eds. 2007. *Best Practices in Literacy Instruction*. New York: Guilford Press.

Hansen, Harlan S., and Ruth M. Hansen. 2010. *Lessons for Literacy: Promoting Preschool Success*. St. Paul, MN: Redleaf Press.

Lee, Kyunghwa, and Mark D. Vagle. 2010. *Developmentalism in Early Childhood and Middle Grades Education: Critical Conversations on Readiness and Responsiveness*. New York: Palgrave Macmillan.

McKenna, Michael C., Sharon Walpole, and Kristin Conradi, eds. 2010. *Promoting Early Reading: Research, Resources, and Best Practices*. New York: Guilford Press.

Nevills, Pamela, and Patricia Wolfe. 2009. *Building the Reading Brain, PreK–3*. Thousand Oaks, CA: Corwin Press.

Petersen, Sandra H., and Donna S. Wittmer. 2009. *Endless Opportunities for Infant and Toddler Curriculum: A Relationship-Based Approach*. Saddle River, NJ: Merrill/Pearson.

Pica, Rae. 2007. *Jump into Literacy: Active Learning for Preschool Children*. Beltsville, MD: Gryphon House.

Soderman, Anne Keil, and Patricia Farrell. 2008. *Creating Literacy-Rich Preschools and Kindergartens*. Boston: Pearson/A&B.

Temple, Charles A., Donna Ogle, Alan N. Crawford, and Penny Freppon. 2005. *All Children Read: Teaching for Literacy in Today's Diverse Classroom*. Boston: Pearson.

US Department of Education. 2005. *Helping Your Child Become a Reader*. Jessup, MD: Education Publications Center.

Weiss, Laura B. 2006. "Brooklyn Reads to Babies." *School Library Journal* 52: 22.

CHAPTER 1

Primary Skills Books

Primary skills books include concept books and picture books that teach basic concepts in an interesting and creative manner. Combining precise and expressive illustrations with limited yet well-chosen words, these books introduce the alphabet, colors, counting, shapes, and spatial and opposites. Concept books are often described as informational books, whereas those containing characters, plots, or dialogue are described as picture books.

Key to Review Sources

BL *Booklist;* **CL** *Children's Literature* (reviews searchable in *Children's Literature Comprehensive Database*); **HBG** *Horn Book Guide;* **HBM** *Horn Book Magazine;* **KR** *Kirkus Reviews;* **LJ** *Library Journal;* **PW** *Publisher's Weekly;* **SLJ** *School Library Journal;* **WLB** *Wilson Library Bulletin*

Some book reviews predate the edition of books because reviews refer to earlier editions.

Alphabet

Azarian, Mary. *A Gardener's Alphabet.* Illustrated by the author. Boston: Houghton Mifflin, 2000.

Watercolors are added to Azarian's signature woodcuts to bring the gardens of this alphabet book to life. With illustrations representing bulbs, compost, nibbling, and the underground, gardening discussions will surely arise, and hopefully children will be inspired to create gardens of their own. (Ages 4–5)

REVIEWS: HBG 09/01/00; SLJ 06/01/00; CL

Bottner, Barbara. *An Annoying ABC.* Illustrated by Michael Emberley. New York: Alfred A. Knopf, 2011.

When Adelaide annoys Bailey, what began as a quiet morning in Miss Mabel's class becomes a chaotic day that each student, from Adelaide to Zelda, will never forget. Energetic mechanical pencil-and-watercolor illustrations provide an additional layer of depth to the amusing yet unruly chain of events. (Ages 3–5)

REVIEWS: HBG 04/01/12; SLJ 10/01/11; KR 08/15/11; PW 07/25/11

Capucilli, Alyssa Satin. *Mrs. McTats and Her Houseful of Cats.* Illustrated by Joan Rankin. New York: Margaret K. McElderry Books, 2001.

Mrs. McTats and Abner, her loving cat, are quite happy living together in their country cottage. Daily scratches on the front door soon provide Mrs. McTats with twenty-five cats, including Basil, Jezebel, Rosebud, and Yodel. The twenty-sixth and final visitor is rather unique but absolutely completes the host of animals residing in the cottage. Both children and adults will appreciate the comical illustrations found in this book of rhymes, letters, and numbers. (Ages 3–5)

REVIEWS: PW 05/24/04; BL 10/01/01; HBG 10/01/01; SLJ 08/01/01; PW 05/28/01; KR 05/01/01; CL

Catalanotto, Peter. *Matthew A.B.C.* Illustrated by the author. New York: Atheneum Books for Young Readers, 2002.

Although Mrs. Tuttle has twenty-five boys in her class named Matthew, she has no problem telling them apart since a letter of the alphabet contributes to the uniqueness of each of them. There's affectionate Matthew, Matthew who's fond of ketchup, perplexed Matthew, and Matthew who is freckled with a rhinoceros, to name a few. When one final boy joins her class, Matthew who's covered in zippers, he is sure to fit in. (Ages 4–5)

REVIEWS: PW 08/15/05; HBG 10/01/02; HBM 07/01/02; BL 07/01/02; SLJ 06/01/02; PW 05/20/02; KR 05/01/02; CL

Cline-Ransome, Lesa. *Quilt Alphabet.* Illustrated by James E. Ransome. New York: Holiday House, 2001.

Using rural America as its backdrop, a picture and poem present clues to the object, plant, or animal chosen to represent each framed, quilted letter. Older preschoolers will enjoy solving the riddles, which range from the very obvious to the slightly abstract. As a convenience to the reader, answers are printed in the back of the book. (Ages 2–5)

REVIEWS: HBG 04/01/02; SLJ 11/01/01; BL 10/01/01; PW 09/17/01; KR 08/01/01; CL

Cronin, Doreen. *Click, Clack, Quackity-Quack.* Illustrated by Betsy Lewin. New York: Atheneum Books for Young Readers, 2005.

The alphabet follows farm animals as they awaken and swiftly prepare for an event. Children will join in the excitement and mystery portrayed in bold, amusing illustrations that lead up to the discovery of a grand picnic in the meadow. (Ages 2–5)

REVIEWS: HBG 01/01/06; SLJ 11/01/05; BL 09/15/05; PW 08/22/05; CL

Demarest, Chris L. *Firefighters A to Z.* Illustrated by the author. New York: Margaret K. McElderry Books, 2000.

Action-filled pastel illustrations and simple, powerful rhymes demonstrate what occurs when a firefighter receives an emergency call. Written by a volunteer firefighter, this educational alphabet book emphasizes the dangers associated with fires and the importance of firefighters. *Firefighters A to Z* is also an appropriate title for observing National Fire Prevention Month in October. (Ages 2–5)

REVIEWS: HBG 04/01/01; SLJ 12/01/00 BL 07/27/00; HBM 07/01/00; CL

Ehlert, Lois. *Eating the Alphabet.* Illustrated by the author. San Diego: Harcourt, 1996.

Lois Ehlert takes readers on a colorful discovery of the alphabet through both common and exotic fruits and vegetables, such as onions, peas, and bananas, as well as *xiguas*, jicamas, and kohlrabies. In addition to learning the alphabet, youngsters will be encouraged by the bold and enticing illustrations to acquaint themselves with both well-known and unfamiliar fruits and vegetables. (Ages 0–3)

REVIEWS: BL 04/01/96; SLJ 05/01/89; PW 03/10/89; CL

Elya, Susan Middleton, and Merry Banks. *N Is for Navidad.* Illustrated by Joe Cepeda. San Francisco: Chronicle Books, 2007.

The Christmas season is celebrated in the tradition of may Latino families as *ángeles* are hung high, sweet *dulces* are prepared, a *nacimiento* is made, and *zapatos* are placed outside. Author notes provide additional information relating to Latino symbols and customs, including pronunciations and definitions for the Spanish words introduced. *N Is for Navidad* is an enlightening cultural experience for non-Latino readers. (Ages 3–5)

REVIEWS: BL 11/01/07; KR 11/01/07; SLJ 10/01/07; CL

Ernst, Lisa Campbell. *The Letters Are Lost!* Illustrated by the author. New York: Puffin Books, 1996.

In this brightly illustrated adventure, preschoolers are challenged to find a set of alphabet blocks that have been scattered and lost. Young readers and listeners will enjoy finding them in an egg carton, in a jack-in-the-box, taking a nap on a quilt, and dancing a jig with a zebra. As the blocks mysteriously disappear again at the end of the book, readers are asked, "Can you guess where they might go?" Responding encourages children to create new adventures of their own. (Ages 2–5)

REVIEWS: HBG 09/01/96; HBM 03/01/96; PW 01/29/96; BL 01/01/96; KR 12/15/95; CL

Ernst, Lisa Campbell. *The Turn-Around, Upside-Down Alphabet Book.* Illustrated by the author. New York: Simon & Schuster Books for Young Readers, 2004.

As the reader turns the book in various directions, letters transform into different objects. The letter *E* becomes an electric plug, the number three, and candles on a birthday cake, while the letter *U* becomes a magnet, a droopy mustache, and a hot dog on a bun. Older preschoolers will be particularly fond of Ernst's abstract illustrations. (Ages 3–5)

REVIEWS: HBG 04/01/05; SLJ 08/01/04; HBM 07/01/04; PW 06/14/04; BL 06/01/04; CL

Fleming, Denise. *Alphabet under Construction.* Illustrated by the author. New York: Henry Holt, 2002.

A hardworking mouse literally constructs the alphabet by folding the *F*, leveling the *L*, quilting the *Q*, and finally, zipping the *Z*. Fleming's book is sure to inspire children to find ways to construct letters of their own. (Ages 2–5)

REVIEWS: PW 07/24/06; HBG 04/01/03; HBM 09/01/02; SLJ 09/01/02; BL 08/01/02; KR 07/01/02; PW 06/24/02; CL

Floca, Brian. *The Racecar Alphabet.* Illustrated by the author. New York: Atheneum Books for Young Readers, 2003.

In a salute to one hundred years of racing, Floca's action-packed alphabet book highlights authentic race cars from the 1901 Ford 999 to the 2001 Ferrari F1-2001. With large pages filled with movement, bold ink-and-watercolor illustrations, and alliterative text like "Vroom—driver versus driver veering, vying, vowing victory," older preschool children, especially race-car enthusiasts, will embrace *Racecar Alphabet.* (Ages 4–5)

REVIEWS: HBG 04/01/04; PW 01/05/04; SLJ 11/01/03; HBM 11/01/03; BL 11/01/03; CL

Freymann, Saxton. *Food for Thought: The Complete Book of Concepts for Growing Minds.* New York: Arthur A. Levine Books, 2005.

Uniquely carved eggplants, leeks, strawberries, squashes, pineapples, and a multitude of other fruits and vegetables are used to teach shapes, colors, numbers, letters, and opposites. Readers will gleefully turn pages as fresh, entertaining food sculptures are presented. (Ages 1–4)

REVIEWS: HBG 10/01/05; SLJ 03/01/05; PW 02/28/05; BL 01/01/05; CL

Geisert, Arthur. *Country Road ABC: An Illustrated Journey through America's Farmland.* Illustrated by the author. New York: Houghton Mifflin Books for Children, 2010.

As readers travel down Iowa's County Road Y31, the beauty of America's rural landscape is alphabetically detailed. With letters representing countryside living, like barn cats, grinding feed, July 4, no mail today, and volunteer fire department, Geisert's book will encourage discussion and be read time and time again. The farm glossary found at the end of the book is well written and reads like a story. (Ages 4–5)

REVIEWS: KR 04/14/10; PW 04/5/10; SLJ 04/01/10; CL

Hoban, Tana. *26 Letters and 99 Cents.* Photographed by the author. New York: Greenwillow Books, 1987.

Hoban's photographs use familiar objects to represent the twenty-six letters of the alphabet. The brightly colored, bold upper- and lowercase letters can also be used to teach color recognition. Although the book's flip side, which uses currency to illustrate numbers from one to ninety-nine, is a little advanced for most preschoolers, new and experienced counters will find the numbers helpful as they learn or master color recognition and number sequences. (Ages 3–5)

REVIEWS: PW 08/07/95; BL 12/15/89; BL 01/15/88; SLJ 04/01/87; BL 03/01/87

Jackson, Woody. *A Cow's Alfalfa-Bet.* Illustrated by the author. Boston: Houghton Mifflin, 2003.

Through serene watercolors, Jackson brings the mountains, lakes, meadows, and valleys of Vermont to life. Black-and-white Holstein cows grace the pages of this book, providing readers a delicate glimpse of flourishing dairy farmlands. Tranquil illustrations make Jackson's book an ideal choice for either naptime or bedtime. (Ages 0–3)

REVIEWS: HBG 04/01/04; PW 09/08/03; SLJ 09/01/03; CL

Jay, Alison. *ABC: A Child's First Alphabet Book.* Illustrated by the author. New York: Dutton Children's Books, 2003.

With the aid of her signature crackle-glaze paintings, Jay creates an alphabet book that not only highlights one significant object for each letter (*M* is for "moon") but also includes several less obvious ones in the same illustration (moose, mountain, and map). Back matter assists in the search by alphabetically listing all items for each letter. (Ages 1–4)

REVIEWS: HBG 04/01/04; BL 10/15/03; SLJ 09/01/03; PW 08/11/03; CL

Kitchen, Bert. *Animal Alphabet.* Illustrated by the author. New York: Dial Books, 1988.

From armadillos, frogs, and lions to ostriches, snails, and zebras, readers are challenged to find and name the animals representing each letter of the alphabet. The layout of this wordless book is simple, but the exquisite illustrations will appeal to all. (Ages 2–5)

REVIEWS: PW 07/29/88

MacDonald, Suse. *A Was Once an Apple Pie.* Adapted and illustrated by the author. New York: Orchard Books, 2005.

From "A was once an apple pie" to "Z was once a little zebra," children will love this modern version of Edward Lear's nineteenth-century poem. With nonsense verses like "skunky, dunky, chunky skunky, stinky, stunky, little skunk," this read-aloud will bring smiles and laughter to all. (Ages 3–5)

REVIEWS: HBG 01/01/06; PW 08/15/05; SLJ 08/01/05; BL 08/01/05; CL

Martin, Bill, Jr., and John Archambault. *Chicka Chicka Boom Boom.* Illustrated by Lois Ehlert. New York: Simon & Schuster, 1989.

The adventure begins when all twenty-six letters of the alphabet race to the top of a coconut tree. Children of all ages will enjoy this colorful rhyming book filled with jazz-flavored phrases like "skit skat skoodle doot," accompanied by the unforgettable refrain, "Chicka chicka boom boom!" Librarians, teachers, and child-care providers should be prepared to read this delightful book again, and again, and again. (Ages 2–5)

REVIEWS: SLJ 06/01/00; BL 03/15/90; BL 10/15/89; PW 10/13/89; BL 10/15/88; CL

Mayer, Bill. *All Aboard! A Traveling Alphabet.* Illustrated by the author. New York: Margaret K. McElderry Books, 2008.

Bill Mayer uses airbrushed, gouache-style illustrations to masterfully conceal letters of the alphabet within travel-related images. Older preschoolers and adults will enjoy hunting for obscured capital letters. To assist with the more intricate images, the last page of the book contains thumbnails of all twenty-six pictures with the hidden letters boldly highlighted. (Ages 3–5)

REVIEWS: BL 03/15/08; SLJ 02/01/08; PW 01/07/08; KR 12/15/07; CL

Murphy, Liz. *ABC Doctor: Staying Healthy from A to Z.* Illustrated by the author. Maplewood, NJ: Blue Apple Books, 2007.

The idea of visiting the doctor terrifies most children. Using friendly illustrations and nonthreatening language, in this book children learn what to expect from a visit to the doctor's office or hospital. Bandages, checkups, otoscopes, stethoscopes, and yes, even urine samples, become less scary after experiencing this book. *ABC Doctor* is a first-rate tool for introducing doctors, nurses, and other health-care professionals to the very young. (Ages 3–5)

REVIEWS: HBG 10/01/07; SLJ 04/01/07; BL 04/01/07; CL

Murray, Alison. *Apple Pie ABC.* Illustrated by the author. New York: Disney-Hyperion Books, 2011.

Adventures begin when a small dog is unable to resist the scrumptious smells of the apple pie his owner is baking. Each new exploit begins with a letter of the alphabet. Children will appreciate the bold capital letters and find the sharp expressive illustrations delightful. (Ages 2–5)

REVIEWS: HBG 10/01/11; SLJ 07/01/11; PW 03/14/11; CL

Pandell, Karen. *Animal Action ABC.* Photographed by Art Wolfe and Nancy Sheehan. New York: Dutton Children's Books, 1996.

This book encourages movement and exercise as children arch their backs and stretch like humpback whales, charge their prey like jaguars, kick like kangaroos, wrestle like two tigers, and zap insects with their tongues like chameleons. Preschoolers of all ages will enjoy imitating the children and animals photographed on the oversize pages, and older children will appreciate the nature notes found in the back matter. (Ages 2–5)

REVIEWS: PW 05/26/03; HBG 03/01/97; BL 11/15/96; PW 10/14/96; KR 09/15/96; CL

Pinto, Sara. *The Alphabet Room.* Illustrated by the author. New York: Bloomsbury, 2003.

As readers turn each page, objects representing each letter of the alphabet are announced and creatively placed in a room. Each time a door within a room is opened, a new, delightful scene is revealed. Intrigue and excitement build as more and more objects are added and the scenes become more outrageous. This charming cumulative book is both simple and complex, which will allow it to be a child's favorite for many years. (Ages 0–5)

REVIEWS: BL 02/01/04; PW 10/27/03; CL

Seeger, Laura Vaccaro. *The Hidden Alphabet.* Illustrated by the author. Brookfield, CT: Roaring Brook Press, 2003.

Pictures surrounded by a black mat and representing letters of the alphabet appear on each page of this book. When readers raise the flaps, each object characterized in this spectacular book transforms into a bold and distinct letter. Older preschoolers will find the unconventional shapes of the letters both challenging and exciting. (Ages 4–5)

REVIEWS: SLJ 10/01/04; HBG 04/01/04; BL 02/01/04; HB 01/01/04; SLJ 11/01/03; PW 09/08/03; KR 08/15/03; CL

Shannon, George. *Tomorrow's Alphabet.* Illustrated by Donald Crews. New York: Greenwillow Books, 1996.

C is for "milk," K is for "tomato," and Q is for "scraps"? Only when you understand that today's milk is tomorrow's cheese, today's tomato is tomorrow's ketchup, and today's scraps are tomorrow's quilt. In this unique concept book, letters represent what everyday objects will become while presenting them in their current form. Sounds confusing? Maybe for some children, but for older preschoolers who have mastered the alphabet, this clever approach will be a delightful challenge. (Ages 4–5)

REVIEWS: HBG 09/01/96; PW 04/01/96; SLJ 04/01/96; BL 03/01/96

Shapiro, Zachary. *We're All in the Same Boat.* Illustrated by Jack E. Davis. New York: G. P. Putnam's Sons, 2009.

It didn't take long for the animals voyaging on Noah's ark to become bored, enraged, impatient, and jittery. As the antsy ants, obnoxious orangutans, worried worms, and others begin to blame Noah, he takes a deep breath and reminds the animals, "We're all in the same boat!" This realization causes the animals to apologize, behave, be neighborly, hold parties, and catch some z's. Shapiro's magnificent ABC book explores emotions and emphasizes the significance of working together. (Ages 3–5)

REVIEWS: BL 01/01/09; SLJ 01/01/09; CL

Sierra, Judy. *The Sleepy Little Alphabet: A Bedtime Story from Alphabet Town.* Illustrated by Melissa Sweet. New York: Alfred A. Knopf, 2009.

In this humorous bedtime tale, it quickly becomes obvious that getting young letters to sleep is a tricky undertaking. Readers and listeners alike will chuckle as twenty-six parents (represented by capital letters) attempt to put their children (lowercase letters) to bed. Whereas q is quiet as a bunny as she colors on her quilt, rambunctious u shocks one of his parents by taking off his underwear. The expressions and shenanigans of these letters will delight children as they become knowledgeable of upper- and lowercase letters. (Ages 2–5)

REVIEWS: BL 07/01/09; HBM 07/01/09; SLJ 06/01/09; PW 05/11/09; CL

Thurlby, Paul. *Paul Thurlby's Alphabet.* Illustrated by the author. Somerville, MA: Templar Books, 2011.

Retro-modern illustrations bring the alphabet alive: *D* is depicted as a dog, two *E*s embrace, a lady dances on an island shaped like *I*, snow-capped mountains form the letter *M*, and the letter *U* goes underground. As the cover states, "Every letter is unforgettable in the awesome ABC book." (Ages 3–5)

REVIEWS: HBG 04/01/12; SLJ 10/01/11; KR 08/15/11; PW 08/15/11; CL

Walton, Rick. *So Many Bunnies: A Bedtime ABC and Counting Book.* Illustrated by Paige Miglio. New York: HarperFestival, 1998.

Classic Victorian-style illustrations by Paige Miglio add a twist to the familiar nursery rhyme "There Was an Old Woman Who Lived in a Shoe." As Old Mother Rabbit puts her twenty-six children to bed, she calls them each by name. From Abel who sleeps on a table to Zed who sleeps on the shed, children will enjoy the rhyme and repetition of the story, as well as the uniqueness of each child. (Ages 3–5)

REVIEWS: PW 12/24/01; HBG 09/01/98; BL 03/15/98; SLJ 03/01/98; KR 02/01/98; CL

Warner, Sharon, and Sarah Forss. *Alphabeasties and Other Amazing Types.* Illustrated by the authors. Maplewood, NJ: Blue Apple Books, 2009.

Letters in various typefaces outline animals in this clever and innovative alphabet book. From the brilliant pullout pages of alligators and giraffes to the one-page interpretations of camels and walruses, this amazing book is a celebration of animals and of both the beauty and the power of typefaces. (Ages 4–5)

REVIEWS: PW 10/26/09; SLJ 10/01/09

Wells, Rosemary. *Max's ABC.* Illustrated by the author. New York: Puffin Books, 2006.

When Max's ants escape from their ant farm, the alphabetic adventure begins. In sequence, each calamity begins with a letter of the alphabet and ends with two or more words representing the letter on each page.

Fans of the bunny siblings Max and Ruby will be thrilled by this adventure's story line and large, bright illustrations. (Ages 2–4)

REVIEWS: HBG 10/01/06; BL 06/01/06; PW 05/29/06; SLJ 05/01/06; HBM 05/01/06; KR 04/15/06; CL

Williams, Laura Ellen. *ABC Kids.* Photographed by the author. New York: Philomel Books, 2000.

Each letter of the alphabet is represented by photographs of boys and girls engaging in activities in ways that only children can. Readers will enjoy viewing the array of expressions found on the faces of children as they enjoy a bubble bath, share a hot dog, settle down for a nap, or encounter a knotted yo-yo. The book's lively photographs and diverse representation of children are sure to bring smiles to all. (Ages 0–3)

REVIEWS: HBG 09/01/00; BL 07/27/00; SLJ 06/12/00; CL

Colors

Carle, Eric. *My Very First Book of Colors.* Illustrated by the author. New York: Philomel Books, 2005.

In this toy and movable book, children are challenged to match pictures on the bottom half of the page with colors on the top half of the page. Levels of difficulty range from simple (brown shoes) to somewhat complex (a multicolored butterfly). (Ages 2–5)

Catalanotto, Peter. *Kitten Red Yellow Blue.* Illustrated by the author. New York: Atheneum Books for Young Readers, 2005.

When Mrs. Tuttle gives sixteen calico kittens to her neighbors, each kitten wears a collar made of ribbon that corresponds to a color representing a unique characteristic of its owner. Red Kitten rescues with the firefighter who drives the red fire engine, Blue Kitten patrols with the police officer wearing a blue uniform, Purple Kitten performs with the musician adorning a purple mohawk, and Pink Kitten practices with the ballerina wearing a pink leotard and ballet slippers. As younger preschoolers learn about colors and community helpers, older children and adults will enjoy the subtle details and humor Catalanotto weaves into the story. (Ages 3–5)

REVIEWS: HBG 10/01/05; SLJ 03/01/05; BL 02/15/05; PW 02/07/05

Charles, N. N. *What Am I? Looking through Shapes at Apples and Grapes.* Illustrated by Leo Dillon and Diane Dillon. New York: Blue Sky Press, 1994.

Die-cuts and rhyming questions teach preschoolers colors, shapes, and fruits. Readers are sure to be astounded as they turn each striking page. (Ages 3–5)

REVIEWS: HBG 03/01/95; SLJ 01/01/95; BL 11/15/94; PW 08/08/94

Dodd, Emma. *Dog's Colorful Day: A Messy Story about Colors and Counting.* Illustrated by the author. New York: Dutton Children's Books, 2000.

By the end of what begins as a normal day, a lovable dog with one black spot on his ear acquires nine additional spots, including a splish of blue paint, a swish of yellow pollen, a splash of gray mud, and a splurt of orange juice. After recapping the dog's assorted spots, Vicky gives him a much-needed bath before he climbs into bed and dreams of his colorful day. Dodd's bold illustrations and bright colors are sure to appeal to preschoolers of various ages. (Ages 2–5)

REVIEWS: PW 12/16/02; HBG 10/01/01; SLJ 03/01/01; BL 02/15/01; PW 01/15/01; KR 11/15/00

Dodds, Dayle Ann. *The Color Box.* Illustrated by Giles Laroche. Boston: Little, Brown, 1992.

Join Alexander, an adventurous monkey, as an ordinary-looking box leads him through worlds of color. As readers turn the pages, die-cuts remind them of previous journeys and provide glimpses of future explorations of black, yellow, orange, blue, red, green, purple, and white. Children will want to rediscover Alexander's travels again and again. (Ages 2–5)

REVIEWS: HBG 09/01/92; SLJ 06/01/92; BL 05/01/92; KR 03/15/92

Ehlert, Lois. *Color Zoo.* Illustrated by the author. New York: J. B. Lippincott, 1989.

Meticulously arranged die-cuts use geometric shapes to bring tigers, monkeys, lions, snakes, and other animals alive. Readers will be captivated as brightly colored faces of animals transform as squares, hexagons, circles, diamonds, and hearts are added and removed. *Color Zoo* is an ideal book for teaching colors, shapes, and animal recognition. An additional notable book by Ehlert that is similar in style is *Color Farm.* (Ages 1–5)

REVIEWS: HBG 09/01/97; BL 03/15/90; BL 05/15/89; SLJ 04/01/89

Ehlert, Lois. *Planting a Rainbow.* Illustrated by the author. New York: Harcourt Brace, 1988.

Primary colors come to life as a child and mother plant their annual flower garden. As red carnations, orange tiger lilies, yellow daisies, blue delphiniums, and purple asters bloom, are picked, and are brought home, most youngsters will be eager to plant gardens of their very own. (Ages 3–5)

REVIEWS: PW 04/07/03; SLJ 05/01/88; BL 04/15/88; PW 03/11/88

Fleming, Denise. *Lunch.* Illustrated by the author. New York: Henry Holt, 1992.

A ravenous mouse stuffs himself on white turnips, yellow corn, blue berries, red apples, and other delicious fruits and vegetables as he scurries across a table. Preschoolers will delight as the mouse gorges himself, growing fatter and leaving a messy trail of colors behind as he hurriedly dashes from one scrumptious, colorful food to the next. (Ages 1–5)

REVIEWS: PW 04/15/96; HBG 03/01/93; BL 11/01/92; KR 10/01/92; PW 09/07/92

Freymann, Saxton. *Food for Thought: The Complete Book of Concepts for Growing Minds.* New York: Arthur A. Levine Books, 2005.

Uniquely carved eggplants, leeks, strawberries, squashes, pineapples, and a multitude of other fruits and vegetables are used to teach shapes, colors, numbers, letters, and opposites. Readers will gleefully turn pages as fresh, entertaining food sculptures are presented. (Ages 1–4)

REVIEWS: HBG 10/01/05; SLJ 03/01/05; PW 02/28/05; BL 01/01/05

Hoban, Tana. *Of Colors and Things.* Photographed by the author. New York: Greenwillow Books, 1989.

Each page of bold photographs is dedicated to a specific color and is filled with familiar objects and foods. From yellow flowers, green cars, and orange pumpkins to blue ribbons, red crayons, and black licorice, young viewers learn and explore basic colors. (Ages 2–5)

REVIEWS: BL 03/15/90; PW 04/14/89; SLJ 04/01/89; BL 04/01/89

Hoban, Tana. *Red, Blue, Yellow Shoe.* Photographed by the author. New York: Greenwillow Books, 1986.

Bold photographs of familiar objects and animals, such as shoes, leaves, teddy bears, and cats, introduce colors to the very young. *Colors Everywhere* is an additional noteworthy title by Hoban. (Ages 0–2)

REVIEWS: SLJ 12/01/96; PW 11/28/86; BL 10/01/86

Holm, Sharon Lane. *Zoe's Hats: A Book of Colors and Patterns.* Honesdale, PA: Boyds Mills Press, 2003.

As Zoe models her favorite hats, including a sailor's cap, a cowboy hat, and yes, even a pair of underwear, readers will chuckle as they learn colors and patterns like spots, stripes, and zigzags. At the end of the book, all hats return and readers are asked to name both their colors and patterns. (Ages 3–5)

REVIEWS: HBG 10/01/03; PW 04/28/03; KR 02/15/03; SLJ 02/15/03; BL 02/01/03

Hubbard, Patricia. *My Crayons Talk.* Illustrated by G. Brian Karas. New York: Henry Holt, 1996.

As a young girl's box of crayons talk, "Yackity. Clackity. Talk. Talk. Talk," purple shouts for bubble gum, blue calls the sky, gold brags, and red roars. Listeners will enjoy chanting along with the short rhythmic rhymes of this book prior to opening a box of crayons and creating their own pictures. (Ages 2–4)

REVIEWS: PW 05/24/99; HBG 09/01/96; SLJ; 05/01/96; BL 04/01/96; KR 03/01/96

Jay, Alison. *Red, Green, Blue: A First Book of Colors.* Illustrated by the author. New York: Dutton Children's Books, 2010.

As children learn colors and are briefly introduced to characters of familiar nursery rhymes, they will enjoy encountering Miss Muffet's black spider, Old Mother Hubbard's orange cupboard, and the golden palace of Old King Cole. With the turn of each page, characters from twenty rhymes come to life and interact with one another thanks to Jay's radiant crackle-varnish illustrations. After reading this delightful book, youngsters will surely want to hear and learn each rhyme in its entirety. (Ages 2–5)

REVIEWS: HBG 10/01/10; SLJ 06/01/10; PW 04/26/10; CL

Jonas, Ann. *Color Dance.* Illustrated by the author. New York: Greenwillow Books, 1989.

> What begins as a simple scarf dance in hues of red, yellow, and blue becomes an artistic lesson in primary and secondary colors. As the three colored scarves are whisked across the stage and later joined by scarves of white, gray, and black, both colors ranging from purple, green, and brown to chartreuse, vermilion, and magenta are created. Back matter includes a color wheel to teach color relationships and encourage children to explore new colors through an array of media, including paints and crayons. (Ages 4–5)
>
> REVIEWS: HBG 03/01/90; SLJ 12/01/89; BL 08/01/89; PW 07/14/89

Jones, Christianne C. *Big Red Farm.* Illustrated by Todd Ouren. Minneapolis: Picture Window Books, 2007.

> As readers visit a farm, they are introduced to red barns, trucks, roosters, ladders, apples, ladybugs, and more. Back matter includes activities, fun facts, and a resource guide for additional books and websites. Other notable books in the Know Your Colors series include *Autumn Orange*, *Camping in Green*, *Hello, Yellow! Purple Pride*, and *Splish, Splash, and Blue*. (Ages 4–5)

Klausmeier, Jesse. *Open This Little Book.* Illustrated by Suzy Lee. San Francisco: Chronicle Books, 2013.

> Preschoolers learn primary colors as ladybugs, frogs, rabbits, and bears open, read, and close books in shades of red, green, orange, yellow, and blue. With each page the books become smaller, but they gradually return to their original size. Youngsters will enjoy the innovative concept of this simple, charming book. (Ages 3–5)
>
> REVIEWS: PW 01/07/13

Letters. New York: PlayBac Publishing USA, 2007.

> Vibrant photographs of animals, plants, and land formations; bold letters; and rhyming text make this nature alphabet book a favorite for older preschoolers. (Ages 4–5)

Lobel, Anita. *One Lighthouse, One Moon.* Illustrated by the author. New York: Greenwillow Books, 2000.

In "All Week Long," the first of three stories within this book, children are introduced to colors and days of the week. With her cat Nini by her side, a young girl wears a varied assortment of shoes, from black sneakers on Monday, red cowboy boots on Tuesday, pink ballet slippers on Saturday, and white dress shoes on Sunday. (Ages 3–5)

REVIEWS: PW 07/08/02; HBG 09/01/00; HBM 07/01/00; SLJ 05/01/00; PW 04/17/00; BL 04/01/00

MacCarthy, Patricia. *Ocean Parade: A Counting Book.* Illustrated by the author. New York: Dial Books for Young Readers, 1990.

In addition to counting from one to one hundred, this book introduces children to colors and shapes through encountering an array of fish and other ocean wonders. (Ages 3–5)

REVIEWS: HBG 09/01/90; SLJ 07/01/90; PW 02/23/90

Martin, Bill, Jr. *Brown Bear, Brown Bear, What Do You See?* Illustrated by Eric Carle. New York: Henry Holt, 1983.

Brown bears, blue horses, purple cats, and black sheep see animals and beautiful children of various colors looking at them. This revision of a 1967 classic blends bold pictures, bright colors, and repetitive text to introduce colors, animals, and rhymes to a broad range of preschoolers. (Ages 2–5)

REVIEWS: HBG 03/01/97; HBG 09/01/92; SLJ 05/01/92; BL 03/01/92

Marzollo, Jean. *I Spy Little Numbers.* Illustrated by Walter Wick. New York: Scholastic, 1999.

In this book, young children will learn numbers, colors, and shapes as they search for objects hidden within the brightly colored photographs. Delightful rhyming text combined with simple and bold illustrations make this a book children will return to again and again. (Ages 2–5)

REVIEWS: CL

McMillan, Bruce. *Growing Colors.* Photographed by the author. New York: Lothrop, Lee, & Shepard Books, 1988.

Brilliant photographs of orange carrots, purple beans, brown peppers, and red potatoes not only introduce readers to colors, fruits, and vegetables but also illustrate how they grow in their natural environment. Young children will be inspired to start gardens and/or experience the taste of the fourteen fruits and vegetables featured. (Ages 3–5)

REVIEWS: BL 01/15/89; BL 09/01/88; SLJ 09/01/88; PW 06/24/88

Otoshi, Kathryn. *One.* Illustrated by the author. San Rafael, CA: KO Kids Books, 2008.

Quiet Blue, Sunny Yellow, Bright Green, Regal Purple, and Outgoing Orange learn lessons of individuality and bullying as Number One teaches them to stand up and say no to Hot Head Red. In what initially appears as a simple, brightly designed color and counting book, both readers and listeners learn essential lessons—everyone is different, and everyone counts. (Ages 3–5)

REVIEWS: SLJ 12/01/08; BL 11/15/08

Petty, Colin. *Colors.* Illustrated by the author. Hauppauge, NY: Barron's Educational Series, 2005.

As children place a finger in a small hole and slide it to the left or right, the answer to the question, "What color?" appears in a cutout box on the corresponding page. As one of the four titles in the Concept Sliders series, *Colors* is an entertaining way to introduce basic colors to youngsters. (Ages 1–3)

REVIEWS: PW 08/28/06

Ranchetti, Sebastiano. *Animals in Color/Animales en color.* Illustrated by the author. Pleasantville, NY: Weekly Reader Books, 2008.

Polar bears, parrots, fish, frogs, flamingos, and other colorful animals assist in teaching colors to preschool children in this simple, informative bilingual book. (Ages 3–5)

Seeger, Laura Vaccaro. *Lemons Are Not Red.* Illustrated by the author. Brookfield, CT: Roaring Book Press, 2004.

Through the use of simple and detailed die-cuts, red lemons magically turn yellow, gray flamingos enchantingly become pink, and blue grass grows to be green. Children will find humor in the initial unnatural colors of well-known items and will be intrigued as the objects materialize into their customary hues. The night fades to black with the final words of the book, "Good night," making Vaccaro's book an ideal bedtime read. (Ages 2–5)

REVIEWS: HBG 04/01/05; HBM 01/01/05; BL 01/01/05; PW 11/15/04; KR 10/01/04

Seuss, Dr. *My Many Colored Days.* Illustrated by Steve Johnson and Lou Fancher. New York: Alfred A. Knopf, 1996.

From feel-good red days when a child kicks up his heels like a horse to purple days when he feels like a sad dinosaur that simply wants to groan and walk alone, rhyming text and dramatic abstract paintings combine colors and animals to introduce emotions to young readers. Written in a style not traditionally associated with Dr. Seuss, this is a book readers will love as they explore and discuss a variety of feelings, moods, and emotions. (Ages 2–5)

REVIEWS: HBG 03/01/97; SLJ 12/01/96; BL 11/01/96; KR 08/15/96; PW 07/22/96

Shahan, Sherry. *Spicy Hot Colors: Colores picantes.* Illustrated by Paula Barragán. Little Rock, AR: August House LittleFolk, 2004

Dazzling illustrations of chili *rojo* sauce, sarapes *anaranjados*, piñatas *moradas*, and guitars *pardos* combined with expressive, jazzy text make Shahan's book a sure delight. In addition to learning colors in both English and Spanish, readers gain a flair for Latino culture. Back matter includes a list of words and phrases that may be unfamiliar to most readers, as well as a pronunciation guide to Spanish words. (Ages 3–6)

REVIEWS: HBG 04/01/05; PW 11/15/04; SLJ 11/01/04; BL 09/15/04

Sidman, Joyce. *Red Sings from Treetops: A Year in Colors.* Illustrated by Pamela Zagarenski. Boston: Houghton Mifflin Books for Children, 2009.

As the seasons change, so do objects represented by familiar colors. Yellow is characterized by goldfinches and flowers in the spring, lemonade and corn in the summer, and school buses in the fall. In the winter, yellow has "gone home" and been replaced by gray and brown. Older preschoolers will adore the award-winning illustrations and gentle story as colors adapt to each season. (Ages 4–5)

REVIEWS: BL 05/01/09; SLJ 04/01/09; HBM 03/01/09; PW 02/16/09; KR 02/01/09

Sís, Peter. *Ballerina!* Illustrated by the author. New York: HarperFestival, 2005.

Colors are explored as a young lover of dance leaps in red leotards, reaches in a yellow turban, dips in a white feather boa, and flutters in her green hat. The foldout finale reconnects the colors, costumes, and dances. *Ballerina!* is an exploration of color, dance, dreams, and imagination. (Ages 3–5)

REVIEWS: HBG 10/01/01; KR 07/20/01; BL 04/01/01; SLJ 04/01/01; PW 03/26/01; KR 03/15/01

Slater, Dashka. *Baby Shoes.* Illustrated by Hiroe Nakata. New York: Bloomsbury Publishing, 2006.

As a young boy enjoys a day of romping around town with his mother, his brand-new white shoes become "speckled, spotted, polka-dotted, puddle-stomping, rainbow-romping" by the end of the day. Both readers and listeners will love the rhymes and rhythm of this book as green grass, purple plums, and brown mud adorn the boy's shoes. (Ages 2–5)

REVIEWS: HBG 10/01/06; SLJ 05/01/06; BL 05/01/06

Spicer, Maggee. *We'll All Go Sailing.* Illustrated by Richard Thompson. Allston, MA: Fitzhenry & Whiteside, 2001.

When the narrator and his friends Maggee and Jesse imagine sailing on seas of blue, black, red, green, and purple, they encounter uniquely colored sea creatures, such as purple sharks, green jellyfish, yellow seahorses, orange barracudas, and pink seals. The rhyming book concludes with its characters creating a book of the things they will see when they go sailing. After taking this colorful journey, readers may enjoy creating of book of their own. (Ages 3–5)

REVIEWS: SLJ 07/01/01; PW 06/04/01; BL 05/15/01

Spurr, Elizabeth. *Farm Life.* Illustrated by Steve Björkman. New York: Holiday House, 2003.

> Barns of red, blue, green, brown, and gray open their doors to reveal the farm equipment and animals that call these structures home. The final dwelling, a white farmhouse, provides a traditional, charming image of rural life. The book's glossary provides definitions to many farming terms that may be unfamiliar to many of today's youth. (Ages 3–5)
>
> REVIEWS: HBG 10/01/03; SLJ 06/01/03; BL 03/15/03; PW 01/20/03

Tafuri, Nancy. *Blue Goose.* Illustrated by the author. New York: Simon & Schuster Books for Young Readers, 2008.

> Blue Goose, Yellow Chick, Red Hen, and White Duck decide to paint their bland farm while Farmer Gray is away. In addition to painting the fence white, the flowers yellow, and the barn red, they blend their hues to create purple, orange, and green for the doors, shutters, grass, and trees. Bright, oversize scenes will appeal to preschoolers as they learn color concepts and the benefits of cooperation. (Ages 1–4)
>
> REVIEWS: SLJ 01/01/08; PW 12/10/07; BL 11/15/07

Tusa, Tricia. *Follow Me.* Illustrated by the author. Boston: Harcourt Children's Books, 2011.

> As a young girl enjoys her swing on a beautiful day, her imagination takes over and transports her to a place filled with pinks, blues, purple, grays, greens, and other colors until she ultimately finds her way back home. (Ages 4–5)
>
> REVIEWS: HBG 10/01/11; SLJ 04/01/11; KR 03/01/11; PW 02/07/11; CL

Van Fleet, Matthew. *One Yellow Lion.* Illustrated by the author. New York: Dial Books for Young Readers, 1992.

> In addition to learning their colors, preschoolers will practice counting from one to ten as each page folds out to reveal lions, squirrels, lizards, alligators, and more. The book ends with a gleeful five-page foldout of all the animals enjoying a day at the shore. (Ages 1–5)
>
> REVIEWS: SLJ 09/01/92; PW 05/25/92

Walsh, Ellen Stoll. *Mouse Paint.* Illustrated by the author. New York: Harcourt Brace Jovanovich, 1989.

> After jumping in jars of red, yellow, and blue paint, three white mice gleefully discover that they can make puddles of orange, green, and purple by combining the hues. The simple cut-paper illustrations are ideal for introducing primary, complementary, and contrasting colors to young children. (Ages 2–5)
>
> REVIEWS: HBG 09/01/96; PW 03/06/95; BL 05/15/89; PW 02/24/89

Watt, Mélanie. *Leon the Chameleon.* Illustrated by the author. Toronto, ON: Kids Can Press, 2001.

> Leon knows he is different because he is unable to blend into his surroundings like the other chameleons. When he stands in green grass, he turns red. When he stands on yellow sand, he turns purple. But after a daylong excursion with the other young chameleons, Leon learns one of the benefits of being unique. In addition to being introduced to primary, complementary, and contrasting colors, children learn the importance of valuing differences. (Ages 2–5)
>
> REVIEWS: HBG 04/01/02; SLJ 04/01/01; BL 04/01/01; KR 02/01/01

Weeks, Sarah. *Counting Ovejas.* Illustrated by David Diaz. New York: Atheneum Books for Young Readers, 2006.

> When a dripping faucet and ticking clock make falling asleep difficult for a young child, he decides to count sheep of various colors. But as more and more sheep enter his bedroom, he must find creative ways to remove them. Bilingual text and subtle, expressive acrylic-and-pencil illustrations make this an unforgettable bedtime story. (Ages 2–4)
>
> REVIEWS: KR 07/01/06; BL 06/01/06; SLJ 06/01/06

Williams, Sue. *I Went Walking.* Illustrated by Julie Vivas. New York: Gulliver Books, 1989.

> A black cat, red cow, pink pig, and yellow dog are just a few of the animals a little boy meets as he begins a walk filled with color and mystery. The story concludes with an amusing two-page spread of the child frolicking

with the six animals following him. As young listeners playfully repeat the rhythmic rhymes, colors and farm animals are identified. (Ages 3–5)

REVIEWS: PW 06/15/92; HBG 03/01/91; SLJ 10/01/90; BL 09/01/90; PW 08/31/90

Wood, Jakki. *Moo, Moo, Brown Cow!* Illustrated by Rog Bonner. Orlando, FL: Harcourt, 1991.

A curious kitten visits Brown Cow, Yellow Goat, Blue Goose, Green Frog, and other mothers living on the farm, inquiring about their young. As readers count from one spotted calf to ten small fries (rainbow trout), they learn lessons of farm animals, including the sounds they make and names of their offspring. (Ages 1–5)

REVIEWS: HBG 09/01/92; SLJ 08/01/92; BL 06/15/92; KR 05/01/92

Counting

Anderson, Sara Lee. *Numbers.* Illustrated by the author. New York: Handprint Books, 2007.

Sturdy, brightly colored graduated-cut pages teach readers to count from one to ten. The simple two-page illustrations dedicated to each number provide an array of objects to count. When preschoolers reach the number seven, for example, they discover seven dots, seven tigers, seven strips on each tiger, seven palm trees, and seven leaves on top of each palm tree. Constructed in a secure rectangular box, this book will be enjoyed by both beginning and experienced counters. (Ages 1–3)

REVIEWS: PW 11/05/07

Anno, Mitsumasa. *Anno's Counting Book.* Illustrated by the author. New York: Thomas Y. Crowell, 1977.

The simple drawings of this multifaceted wordless counting book depict the seasonal changes and growth of a rural area over the course of twelve months. For example, in the fourth month, spring is clearly in bloom as four children play in a field covered in colorful flowers. Additionally, readers will observe four green trees on the hillside, four fish swimming in a brook, a woman feeding her four pigs, and four geese flying above in the blue sky. The back matter of this timeless book includes author notes relating to numbers. (Ages 3–5)

Baker, Keith. *Potato Joe.* Illustrated by the author. Orlando: Harcourt, 2008.

As Potato Joe begins the count, ten lively potatoes count from one to ten and back again. As they play tic-tac-toe, get frightened by a huge black crow, get covered in snow, and swing their partner and do-si-do, they are joined by two garden friends, Tomato Flo and Watermelon Moe, before they return safely to the rich brown dirt for a snooze. The catchy text, based on the familiar nursery rhyme "One Potato, Two Potato," will quickly become a read-aloud favorite. (Ages 3–5)

REVIEWS: PW 06/16/08; SLJ 06/01/08; KR 05/01/08; CL

Bang, Molly. *Ten, Nine, Eight.* Illustrated by the author. New York: Tupelo Books, 1996.

The reader counts from ten to one as a father prepares his daughter for bed. The award-winning illustrations depict the warmth of a child's room (soft toys, snow falling through open windowpanes, and a mobile made of beautiful shells) and the wonder of love shared between a father and daughter. This book is sure to be a bedtime favorite. (Ages 2–4)

REVIEWS: BL 11/15/98; PW 05/03/91; BL 12/15/89; CL

Bateman, Donna M. *Deep in the Swamp.* Illustrated by Brian Lies. Watertown, MA: Charlesbridge, 2007.

While counting the young of mother river otters, snapping turtles, blue herons, rat snakes, crayfish, and more, children learn about the sounds, plants, and animals of the Okefenokee Swamp. The "Swamp Flora and Fauna Facts" section at the back of the book provides pictures and additional details. (Ages 3–5)

REVIEWS: HBG 10/01/07; BL 05/15/07; SLJ 03/01/07; PW 01/15/07; KR 01/01/07; CL

Capucilli, Alyssa Satin. *Mrs. McTats and Her Houseful of Cats.* Illustrated by Joan Rankin. New York: Margaret K. McElderry Books, 2001.

Mrs. McTats and Abner, her loving cat, are quite happy living together in their country cottage. Daily scratches on the front door soon provide Mrs. McTats with twenty-five cats, including Basil, Jezebel, Rosebud, and Yodel. The twenty-sixth and final visitor is rather unique but absolutely completes the host of animals residing in the cottage. Both children and adults will appreciate the comical illustrations found in this book of rhymes, letters, and numbers. (Ages 3–5)

REVIEWS: PW 05/24/04; BL 10/01/01; HBG 10/01/01; SLJ 08/01/01; PW 05/28/01; KR 05/01/01; CL

Cronin, Doreen. *Click, Clack, Splish, Splash: A Counting Adventure.* Illustrated by Betsy Lewin. New York: Atheneum Books for Young Readers, 2006.

When a farmer falls asleep on the sofa, his animals embark on a unique fishing adventure. As children enjoy the delightful expressions on the faces of the duck, chickens, cows, fish, and other creatures, they learn to count from one to ten and from ten to one. (Ages 2–5)

REVIEWS: HBG 10/01/06; KR 01/01/06; BL 01/01/06; SLJ 01/01/06; PW 11/21/05; CL

Dahl, Michael. *Pie for Piglets: Counting by Twos.* Illustrated by Todd Ouren. Minneapolis: Picture Window Books, 2005.

Join two hungry piglets who count by twos as they fill a pie with creamy butter, cobs of corn, cinnamon rolls, pineapple pizza, and other unconventional ingredients. The back matter of this educational counting book includes fun facts about pigs, safe web resources, and a game that challenges children to find numbers hidden throughout the book. *Lots of Ladybugs! Counting by Fives* is another notable title by Dahl and Ouren in the Know Your Numbers series. (Ages 4–5)

REVIEWS: SLJ 06/01/05; CL

Dodd, Emma. *Dog's Colorful Day: A Messy Story about Colors and Counting.* Illustrated by the author. New York: Dutton Children's Books, 2000.

By the end of what begins as a normal day, a lovable dog with one black spot on his ear acquires nine additional spots, including a splish of blue paint, a swish of yellow pollen, a splash of gray mud, and a splurt of orange juice. After recapping the dog's assorted spots, Vicky gives him a much-needed bath before he climbs into bed and dreams of his colorful day. Dodd's bold illustrations and bright colors are sure to appeal to preschoolers of various ages. (Ages 2–5)

REVIEWS: PW 12/16/02; HBG 10/01/01; SLJ 03/01/01; BL 02/15/01; PW 01/15/01; KR 11/15/00

Ehlert, Lois. *Fish Eyes: A Book You Can Count On.* Illustrated by the author. New York: Red Wagon Books, 1990.

> After imagining being a fish, children are taken on an underwater journey, where they see and count a variety of brightly colored fish. Ehlert's rhyming counting book will amuse early counters. (Ages 3–5)
>
> REVIEWS: PW 06/15/92; HBG 09/01/90; SLJ 05/01/90; PW 04/13/90; BL 03/01/90; CL

Falconer, Ian. *Olivia Counts.* Illustrated by the author. New York: Atheneum Books for Young Readers, 2002.

> Toddlers will enjoy counting from one to ten with Olivia, a charming piglet. In bold three-color illustrations, children will join Olivia as she counts balls, aunts, books, toys, and more. The book concludes with ten Olivias engaging in activities like jumping rope, hammering a nail, wearing panty hose, and performing a handstand. (Ages 0–3)
>
> REVIEWS: HBG 10/01/02; BL 07/01/02; SLJ 06/01/02; PW 05/06/02; KR 05/01/02; CL

Falwell, Cathryn. *Turtle Splash! Countdown at the Pond.* Illustrated by the author. New York: Greenwillow Books, 2001.

> Ten turtles are startled by the bullfrogs, deer, butterflies, and mosquitoes they encounter as they lounge on a log at the pond. In addition to counting from ten to one, preschoolers will discover animals living in ponds and woodlands. The back matter includes detailed information relating to the animals appearing in the book and instructions for making leaf prints. (Ages 3–5)
>
> REVIEWS: HBG 04/01/02; SLJ 09/01/01; BL 08/01/01; PW 07/09/01; KR 07/01/01; CL

Fleming, Denise. *The First Day of Winter.* Illustrated by the author. New York: Henry Holt, 2005.

> In the tradition of "The Twelve Days of Christmas," an African-American boy uses one red cap with a gold snap, three striped scarves, five birdseed pockets, seven maple leaves, and other items to build a snowman during the first ten days of winter. Children who know the traditional Christmas song will sing along as they count to ten and back again. (Ages 3–5)
>
> REVIEWS: HBG 01/01/06; BL 12/15/05; SLJ 12/01/05; HBM 11/01/05; PW 09/26/05; CL

Franco, Betsy. *Birdsongs.* Illustrated by Steve Jenkins. New York: Margaret K. McElderry Books, 2007.

As they count from ten to one, preschoolers will enjoy learning the unique sounds of woodpeckers, sparrows, chickadees, crows, humming-birds, and other fascinating birds. As night falls and a day filled with searching for breakfast bugs, crowding around bird feeders, and tottering along fences come to a quiet end, a mockingbird begins to sing, copying all of the songs heard over the course of the day. The back matter includes interesting "feathery facts" on the eleven birds beautifully collaged throughout the book. (Ages 3–5)

REVIEWS: HBG 10/01/07; BL 01/01/07; SLJ 01/01/07; PW 12/11/06; CL

Freymann, Saxton. *Food for Thought: The Complete Book of Concepts for Growing Minds.* New York: Arthur A. Levine Books, 2005.

Uniquely carved eggplants, leeks, strawberries, squashes, pineapples, and a multitude of other fruits and vegetables are used to teach shapes, colors, numbers, letters, and opposites. Readers will gleefully turn pages as fresh, entertaining food sculptures are presented. (Ages 1–4)

REVIEWS: HBG 10/01/05; SLJ 03/01/05; PW 02/28/05; BL 01/01/05; CL

Gorbachev, Valeri. *Christopher Counting.* Illustrated by the author. New York: Philomel Books, 2008.

Young Christopher Rabbit loves to count. He counts all day at school—everything in his backpack; the boots, shoes, and sneakers in the hallway; lilies in the pond; and the number of baskets the herons and beavers score during a basketball game. Preschoolers will enjoy counting along with Christopher, but they will also discover many additional characters and objects to count between the pages of this fun read-aloud. (Ages 3–5)

REVIEWS: PW 03/17/08; SLJ 03/01/08; KR 03/01/08; CL

Hayes, Sarah. *Nine Ducks Nine.* Illustrated by the author. New York: Lothrop, Lee, & Shepard Books, 1990.

Nine watchful ducks realize that a wily fox is trailing them as they enjoy a walk on a sunny day. One by one, the shrewd ducks break away, leading the fox down to the rickety bridge. Pastoral watercolors and humorous speech balloons add further appeal to this amusing, rhyming counting book. (Ages 3–5)

REVIEWS: PW 02/19/96; HBG 03/01/91; SLJ 12/01/90; PW 10/12/90; PW 10/2/90

Hines, Anna Grossnickle. *1, 2, Buckle My Shoe.* Illustrated by the author. Orlando, FL: Harcourt, 2008.

A familiar nursery rhyme, combined with quilt patches detailed with buttons and bold numbers, makes this a memorable counting book for preschoolers. (Ages 1–3)

REVIEWS: BL 05/15/08; SLJ 05/01/08; KR 04/15/08; CL

Hoban, Tana. *1, 2, 3.* Photographed by the author. New York: Greenwillow Books, 1985.

Bold photographs of familiar objects such as shoes, blocks, fingers, and animal crackers are used to introduce the very young to numbers and the concept of counting. (Ages 0–2)

Jay, Alison. *1, 2, 3: A Child's First Counting Book.* Illustrated by the author. New York: Dutton Children's Books, 2007.

As children count to ten and back again, they encounter characters from more than fifteen of their favorite fairy tales, including "Cinderella," "The Princess and the Pea," "Hansel and Gretel," "The Gingerbread Man," and "Jack and the Beanstalk." Jay's magnificent crackle-glaze paintings breathe life into each word and fairy tale. (Ages 1–5)

REVIEWS: BL 09/15/07; PW 09/03/07; SLJ 09/01/07; CL

Krebs, Laurie. *We All Went on Safari: A Counting Journey through Tanzania.* Illustrated by Julia Cairns. Cambridge, MA: Barefoot Books, 2003.

Readers will count animals in both English and Swahili as they join a group of Maasai children walking through the grasslands, lakes, and rocky hillside glens of Tanzania. Back pages include detailed information of Tanzania, the Maasai people, Swahili names, and counting in Swahili. (Ages 3–5)

REVIEWS: HBG 10/01/03; SLJ 04/01/03; PW 03/24/03; CL

Leuck, Laura. *One Witch.* Illustrated by S. D. Schindler. New York: Walker & Company, 2003.

Realizing that her cauldron is empty, a witch borrows enough ingredients from her friends to make a gruesome brew. As children count from one to ten, then back to one, they will enjoy meeting cats, goblins, skeletons, and other bizarre creatures invited to feast with the gracious witch. *One Witch* is an eerie yet amusing Halloween story. (Ages 3–5)

REVIEWS: HBG 04/01/04; BL 09/01/03; PW 08/04/03; SLJ 08/01/03; CL

Ljungkvist, Laura. *Follow the Line.* Illustrated by the author. New York: Viking, 2006.

As readers follow a line through cities, oceans, skies, forests, and villages, they encounter and count orange buildings, people with curly hair, ambulances, traffic signs shaped like circles, striped sails on ships, dragonflies, and fences. In addition to counting, preschoolers will search for details; build their vocabulary; and learn colors, patterns, and shapes. (Ages 4–5)

REVIEWS: HBG 10/01/06; PW 05/15/06; SLJ 05/01/06; KR 04/15/06: CL

Lobel, Anita. *One Lighthouse, One Moon.* Illustrated by the author. New York: Greenwillow Books, 2000.

In "One Lighthouse, One Moon," one of three stories in the pages of this book, children are invited to join Nini, an observant cat, for a seaside counting adventure that includes lighthouses, sailors, pelicans, geese, stars, and yes, the moon. (Ages 3–5)

REVIEWS: PW 07/08/02; HBG 09/01/00; HBM 07/01/00; SLJ 05/01/00; PW 04/17/00; BL 04/01/00; CL

MacCarthy, Patricia. *Ocean Parade: A Counting Book.* Illustrated by the author. New York: Dial Books for Young Readers, 1990.

In addition to counting from one to one hundred, this book introduces children to colors and shapes through encountering an array of fish and other ocean wonders. (Ages 3–5)

REVIEWS: HBG 09/01/90; SLJ 07/01/90; PW 02/23/90

MacDonald, Suse. *Look Whooo's Counting.* Illustrated by the author. New York: Scholastic, 2000.

Young Owl learns to count as she flies through the night sky and encounters animals on hills, in the grass, on trees, and among flowers. Children with advanced number recognition abilities will be in awe as they discover that the number representing each cut-paper animal is visually formed in the animal's body (such as the tails of the mice form the number two, the horns on the sheep resemble the number six). Counters of all ages will enjoy this imaginative book. (Ages 3–5)

REVIEWS: HBG 04/01/01; SLJ 12/01/00; PW 10/16/00; BL 10/15/00; KR 10/01/00

Mannis, Celeste D. *One Leaf Rides the Wind: Counting in a Japanese Garden.* Illustrated by Susan Hartung. New York: Puffin Books, 2002.

Japanese culture, numbers, and poetry unify flawlessly as readers count temple dogs, roofs on a pagoda, sweet surprises on a lacquered tray, and glittering koi with a young girl adorned in a traditional Japanese kimono. As each number is introduced, brilliant haikus and brief notes provide enchanting insight on Japanese philosophy, culture, and religion. (Ages 4–6)

REVIEWS: HBG 04/01/03; SLJ 10/01/02; PW 09/02/02; KR 08/01/02; CL

Martin, Bill, Jr. *Ten Little Caterpillars.* Illustrated by Lois Ehlert. New York: Beach Lane Books, 2011.

Readers count from one to ten as multiple species of caterpillars crawl, wriggle, climb, and fall across the pages. In addition to counting, children learn the names of popular caterpillars and explore the animals, plants, and flowers living within their ecosystems. Readers will especially enjoy discovering what each caterpillar will metamorphose into when it becomes an adult. (Ages 2–5)

REVIEWS: HBG 04/01/12; SLJ 08/01/11; KR 07/15/11; PW 05/30/11; CL

Martin, Bill, Jr., and Michael Sampson. *Chicka Chicka 1, 2, 3.* Illustrated by Lois Ehlert. New York: Simon & Schuster Books for Young Readers, 2004.

As numbers one to ninety-nine race to the top of the apple tree, zero wonders, "Will there be a place for me?" Although the other numbers ignore zero as they romp and play, a swarm of bees make him a hero and prove that each number has a special place. As readers count from one to one hundred, they will enjoy the bold, colorful illustrations as well as the rhythm of the rhymes. (Ages 3–5)

REVIEWS: HBG 04/01/05; HBM 09/01/04; SLJ 08/01/04; PW 07/19/04; BL 06/01/04; CL

Marzollo, Jean. *I Spy Little Numbers.* Illustrated by Walter Wick. New York: Scholastic, 1999.

In this book, young children will learn numbers, colors, and shapes as they search for objects hidden within the brightly colored photographs. Delightful rhyming text combined with simple and bold illustrations make this a book children will return to again and again. (Ages 2–5)

REVIEWS: CL

McFarland, Lyn Rossiter. *Mouse Went Out to Get a Snack.* Illustrated by Jim McFarland. New York: Farrar, Straus, & Giroux, 2005.

When a hungry little mouse leaves his hole in search of a snack, he discovers a table filled with more delicious foods than he could have ever dreamed of. Youngsters of all ages will enjoy counting to ten as he fills his plate with cheese, baby carrots, ears of corn, colorful cupcakes, and other scrumptious treats. When the mouse encounters a cat, readers will have the pleasure of counting from ten to one. (Ages 2–5)

REVIEWS: HBG 10/01/05; SLJ 03/01/05; CL

Morozumi, Atsuko. *One Gorilla: A Counting Book.* Illustrated by the author. New York: Farrar, Straus, & Giroux, 1990.

With the assistance of a mild-mannered gorilla, children will enjoy searching the pages of this delightful book for animals that the narrator loves. From budgerigars in the house to cats in the garden, this delicately drawn work has all the elements of a dearly loved bedtime story. (Ages 3–5)

REVIEWS: HBG 03/01/91; SLJ 01/01/91; BL 11/01/90

Numbers. Illustrated by Fiona Land. New York: Ladybird Books, 2008.

As young children touch and feel soft caterpillars, bumpy frogs, furry cats, and more, they also learn to count from one to five. (Ages 0–2)

Nunn, Daniel. *Counting 1 to 10.* Illustrated by Joanna Hinton-Malivoire. Chicago: Raintree, 2012.

Bright and bold illustrations and photographs of cupcakes, sunflowers, seashells, ducklings, striped socks, birthday candles, parrots, kites, and more entertain readers as they count from one to ten. In addition to a table of contents and index, this basic counting book includes a counting challenge young readers are sure to enjoy. (Ages 3–5)

REVIEWS: SLJ 04/01/12; CL

Otoshi, Kathryn. *One.* Illustrated by the author. San Rafael, CA: KO Kids Books, 2008.

Quiet Blue, Sunny Yellow, Bright Green, Regal Purple, and Outgoing Orange learn lessons of individuality and bullying as Number One teaches them to stand up and say no to Hot Head Red. In what initially appears as a simple, brightly designed color and counting book, both readers and listeners learn essential lessons—everyone is different, and everyone counts. (Ages 3–5)

REVIEWS: SLJ 12/01/08; BL 11/15/08; CL

Ranchetti, Sebastiano. *Counting with Animals.* Illustrated by the author. Pleasantville, NY: Weekly Reader Books, 2008.

Monkeys, frogs, porcupines, salamanders, penguins, and other colorful animals assist in teaching counting and animal recognition skills in this simple, informative concept book. (Ages 2–4)

REVIEWS: CL

Reiser, Lynn. *Hardworking Puppies.* Illustrated by the author. Orlando: Harcourt, 2006.

As ten eager puppies find jobs with firefighters, clowns, sled drivers, hospital volunteers, and security officers, children are introduced to subtraction and learn about many important roles that dogs often play in the community. "Paw Notes" at the end of the book provides additional information relating to guard dogs, water-rescue dogs, performing dogs, assistance dogs, and more. (Ages 3–5)

REVIEWS: HBG 10/01/06; BL 06/01/06; PW 05/29/06; HBM 05/01/06; SLJ 04/01/06; CL

Reiser, Lynn. *Ten Puppies.* Illustrated by the author. New York: Greenwillow Books, 2003.

With the aid of a dog and her adopted puppies, readers learn to count to ten in multiple ways. Each page categorizes puppies by unique traits, including tongues (pink or blue), ears (floppy or perky), tails (curly or straight), fur (shaggy or smooth), and paws (little or small), and young-sters are encouraged to count the number of puppies in each group. In the end, however, all ten share one common characteristic—they grow up to become dogs. (Ages 3–5)

REVIEWS: HBG 10/01/03; PW 05/26/03; HBM 05/01/03; SLJ 04/01/03; KR 03/15/03; CL

Root, Phyllis. *One Duck Stuck.* Illustrated by Jane Chapman. Cambridge, MA: Candlewick Press, 1998.

When a duck gets "stuck in the muck" down by the marsh, neighbor-ing crickets, frogs, snails, snakes, and others respond to the call for help. As children listen to the sounds, rhythms, and rhymes of this whimsical tale, they will not be able to resist participating and chant-ing repeated phrases like "Help! Help! Who can help?" and "We can! We can!" (Ages 2–5)

REVIEWS: PW 01/20/03; HBG 09/01/98; SLJ 06/01/98; PW 05/04/98; CL

Schachner, Judy. *Skippyjon Jones 1-2-3.* Illustrated by the author. New York: Dutton Children's Books, 2008.

Children will enjoy counting big ears, nosy sisters, fuzzy piñatas, rolls of toilet tissue, and more with America's favorite Siamese kitty boy. The back matter teaches children to count from one to ten in both English and Spanish. (Ages 3–5)

REVIEWS: PW 12/17/07; CL

Seeger, Laura Vaccaro. *One Boy.* Illustrated by the author. New York: Roar-ing Brook, 2008.

Rhymes, die-cuts, and vibrant and simple drawings bring the numbers one to ten alive in this award-winning book. Seeger adeptly weaves the relationship of words within words as a boy creates ten distinctive paint-ings. A broad audience from early counters to beginner readers will appreciate this work. (Ages 2–5)

REVIEWS: BL 10/15/08; SLJ 10/01/08; PW 07/07/08; CL

Sierra, Judy. *Counting Crocodiles.* Illustrated by Will Hillenbrand. San Diego: Gulliver Books, 1997.

Based on an Asian trickster folktale, a sly monkey uses her ability to count to ten and back to one to trick a sea of crocodiles. As she counts, naive crocodiles form a bridge, allowing the monkey to journey from her lemon-tree island to an island flourishing with bananas. A fine blend of humor, movement, and rhyming verse crafts a book certain to be a read-aloud favorite. (Ages 3–5)

REVIEWS: PW 10/01/01; HBG 03/01/98; SLJ 10/01/97; BL 09/01/97; PW 06/30/97; CL

Silverman, Erica. *The Halloween House.* Illustrated by Jon Agee. New York: Farrar, Straus, & Giroux, 1997.

As two escaped prisoners take refuge in an old mansion on Halloween night, they encounter many spooky creatures occupying the house. Children will enjoy counting the rising vampires, swooping bats, dancing skeletons, and swinging spiders throughout the year. (Ages 3–5)

REVIEWS: PW 09/27/99; HBG 03/01/98; SLJ 11/01/97; HBM 09/01/97; BL 09/01/97; KR 07/01/97; CL

Sís, Peter. *Fire Truck.* Illustrated by the author. New York: Greenwillow Books, 2004.

Matt loves fire trucks. He is so fascinated by fire trucks that he dreams he became one. Youngsters will enjoy counting Matt's ladders, flashing lights, sirens, boots, and more. (Ages 3–5)

REVIEWS: BL 09/15/98; HBM 09/01/98; SLJ 09/01/98; KR 08/01/98; CL

Slaughter, Tom. *1, 2, 3.* Illustrated by the author. Plattsburgh, NY: Tundra Books, 2003.

Bold, familiar objects like eyeglasses, buttons, fish, beach balls, and apple trees against solid backgrounds will make this counting book a favorite of a various range of preschoolers. For example, early counters may simply identify nine buildings; more advanced children may realize that each building also has nine windows. Because Tom Slaughter's art has been exhibited in modern galleries around the country, *1, 2, 3* also doubles as a book of art for young children. (Ages 2–5)

REVIEWS: PW 12/12/05; PW 11/17/03; SLJ 11/01/03; CL

Spurr, Elizabeth. *Farm Life.* Illustrated by Steve Björkman. New York: Holiday House, 2003.

While counting balers, threshers, stallions, bales of hay, heifers, and piglets, children are introduced to the charms of traditional farm life.

The book's glossary provides definitions to farming terms that are likely unfamiliar to many of today's youth. (Ages 3–5)

REVIEWS: HBG 10/01/03; SLJ 06/01/03; BL 03/15/03; PW 01/20/03; CL

Van Fleet, Matthew. *One Yellow Lion.* Illustrated by the author. New York: Dial Books for Young Readers, 1992.

In addition to learning their colors, preschoolers will practice counting from one to ten as each page folds out to reveal lions, squirrels, lizards, alligators, and more. The book ends with a gleeful five-page foldout of all the animals enjoying a day at the shore. (Ages 1–5)

REVIEWS: SLJ 09/01/92; PW 05/25/92; CL

Wadsworth, Olive A. *Over in the Meadow: A Counting Rhyme.* Illustrated by Anna Vojtech. New York: North-South Books, 2002.

The sounds and behaviors of meadow animals provide the backdrop for Vojtech's rendition of this familiar nineteenth-century rhyme. Children will enjoy counting from one to ten as turtles dig, rats gnaw, crows caw, and lizards bask. Older readers will delight in discovering ants, bugs, leaves, geese, and other countable animals and items nestled in the background. Ezra Jack Keats's *Over in the Meadow* (1999) is also a notable adaptation of the rhyme. (Ages 3–5)

REVIEWS: PW 08/25/03; HBG 10/01/02; SLJ; 04/01/02; KR 02/01/02; CL

Walsh, Ellen Stoll. *Mouse Count.* Illustrated by the author. San Diego: Harcourt Brace Jovanovich, 1991.

As a hungry snake discovers ten sleeping mice, he counts each one before adding them to the jar he hopes to fill for dinner. Greed gets the best of the snake, however, and the clever mice outwit him, "uncount" themselves, and run home safely. In addition to being an engaging counting story, the book teaches two very important lessons. (Ages 2–5)

REVIEWS: HBG 09/01/96; PW 03/06/95; HBG 09/01/91; SLJ 05/01/91; BL 02/15/91; PW 01/25/91; CL

Walton, Rick. *So Many Bunnies: A Bedtime ABC and Counting Book.* Illustrated by Paige Miglio. New York: HarperFestival, 1998.

Classic Victorian-style illustrations by Paige Miglio add a twist to the familiar nursery rhyme "There Was an Old Woman Who Lived in a

Shoe." As Old Mother Rabbit puts her twenty-six children to bed, she calls them each by name. From Abel who sleeps on a table to Zed who sleeps on the shed, children will enjoy the rhyme and repetition of the story, as well as the uniqueness of each child. (Ages 3–5)

REVIEWS: PW 12/24/01; HBG 09/01/98; BL 03/15/98; SLJ 03/01/98; KR 02/01/98; CL

Weeks, Sarah. *Counting Ovejas.* Illustrated by David Diaz. New York: Atheneum Books for Young Readers, 2006.

When a dripping faucet and ticking clock make falling asleep difficult for a young child, he decides to count sheep of various colors. But as more and more sheep enter his bedroom, he must find creative ways to remove them. Bilingual text and subtle, expressive acrylic-and-pencil illustrations make this an unforgettable bedtime story. (Ages 2–4)

REVIEWS: KR 07/01/06; BL 06/01/06; SLJ 06/01/06; CL

Wells, Rosemary. *Max Counts His Chickens.* Illustrated by the author. New York: Penguin, 2007.

Max makes a mess as he and his sister, Ruby, search the house for ten pink marshmallow chicks left by the Easter Bunny. Children will enjoy the contrast between Ruby's pursuits in very rational locations like her dollhouse and on the pantry shelf and Max's illogical rummages through a tube of toothpaste and an orange juice carton. (Ages 3–5)

REVIEWS: HBG 10/01/07; SLJ 02/01/07; PW 01/29/07; BL 01/01/07; CL

Wood, Audrey. *Ten Little Fish.* Illustrated by Bruce Wood. New York: Blue Sky Press, 2004.

Ten brightly colored fish disappear one by one from the pages of this digitally created three-dimensional book as they dive, hide, grab a snack, and make a friend. Children with a complete understanding of the numbers one through ten will enjoy the *Finding Nemo*–like characters in this descending counting book. (Ages 4–5)

REVIEWS: HBG 04/01/05; SLJ 10/01/04; BL 08/01/04; PW 07/19/04

Wood, Jakki. *Moo, Moo, Brown Cow!* Illustrated by Rog Bonner. Orlando, FL: Harcourt, 1991.

A curious kitten visits Brown Cow, Yellow Goat, Blue Goose, Green Frog, and other mothers living on the farm, inquiring about their young. As readers count from one spotted calf to ten small fries (rainbow trout), they learn lessons of farm animals, including the sounds they make and names of their offspring. (Ages 1–5)

REVIEWS: HBG 09/01/92; SLJ 08/01/92; BL 06/15/92; KR 05/01/92; CL

Wormell, Christopher. *Teeth, Tales, and Tentacles: An Animal Counting Book.* Illustrated by the author. Philadelphia: Running Press, 2004.

As older preschoolers count opossum babies, bear claws, caterpillar segments, rings on a lemur, and leopard rosettes, they will be enthralled by bold linocut illustrations of the twenty animals represented in this complex counting book. To encourage further exploration, miniature block prints and fascinating facts of the featured animals are found in the rear of the book. (Ages 4–5)

REVIEWS: HBG 04/01/05; BL 10/01/04; PW 08/23/04; KR 07/15/04; CL

Yektai, Niki. *Bears at the Beach: Counting 10 to 20.* Illustrated by the author. Minneapolis: Millbrook Press, 1996.

As eleven bears enjoy a fun-filled day at the beach, readers will enjoy counting umbrellas, towels, shells, pails, and sand castles. Yektai's book is perfect for children who have mastered counting from one to ten and are ready to move ahead with numbers ten to twenty. (Ages 3–5)

REVIEWS: HBG 09/01/96; BL 07/01/96; SLJ 06/01/96; PW 01/22/96: CL

Young, Cybèle. *Ten Birds.* Illustrated by the author. Tonawanda, NY: Kids Can Press, 2011.

Ten birds, with names like Brilliant, Magnificent, Extraordinary, Highly Satisfactory, and Remarkable, need to get from one side of the river to the other. Nine birds use resources such as pulleys, wind machines, balloons, mechanical wings, and catapults to build elaborate and somewhat dangerous devices to cross. The last bird to cross, the one oddly dubbed "Needs Improvement," simply walks across the existing bridge. Readers will appreciate the intricate pen-and-ink drawings as they count from ten to one. (Ages 4–5)

REVIEWS: HBG 10/01/11; PW 04/18/11; SLJ 04/01/11; KR 02/15/11; CL

Zelinsky, Paul O. *Knick-Knack Paddywhack!* Illustrated by the author. New York: Dutton Children's Books, 2002

In this skillfully crafted toy and movable adaptation of the well-known folk song, readers of all ages will marvel at the animation experienced through pulling tabs, lifting and turning flaps, and spinning wheels. Children will count, laugh, clap, and sing for hours as these old men come rolling home. (Ages 2–5)

REVIEWS: HBG 04/01/03; HBM 01/01/03; SLJ 12/01/02; BL 11/01/02; KR 08/15/02; PW 08/12/02; CL

Shapes

Blackstone, Stella. *Bear in a Square.* Illustrated by Debbie Harter. Brooklyn, NY: Barefoot Books, 1998.

This book challenges readers to find squares, circles, stars, and other shapes hidden in pools, caves, around clowns, and in other exciting locations. The back matter includes a picture of the gleeful bear surrounded by each shape featured in the book. (Ages 3–5)

REVIEWS: BL 10/01/98; SLJ 10/01/98; KR 08/01/98; CL

Carle, Eric. *My Very First Book of Shapes.* Illustrated by the author. New York: Philomel Books, 2005.

In this toy and movable book, children are challenged to match pictures on the bottom half of the page with corresponding shapes on the top half of the page. Levels of difficulty range from simple circles and squares to somewhat complex shapes such as squiggles and crescents. (Ages 2–5)

REVIEWS: PW 04/25/05; CL

Charles, N. N. *What Am I? Looking through Shapes at Apples and Grapes.* Illustrated by Leo Dillon and Diane Dillon. New York: Blue Sky Press, 1994.

Die-cuts and rhyming questions teach preschoolers colors, shapes, and fruits. Readers are sure to be astounded as they turn each striking page. (Ages 3–5)

REVIEWS: HBG 03/01/95; SLJ 01/01/95; BL 11/15/94; PW 08/08/94; CL

Cleary, Brian P. *Windows, Rings, and Grapes: A Look at Different Shapes.* Illustrated by Brian Gable. Minneapolis: Millbrook Press, 2009.

Rhyming text and humorous cartoon drawings are used to provide detailed descriptions of ovals, triangles, rectangles, squares, and circles. Older preschoolers with a desire to move beyond shape basics will find this book refreshing. (Ages 4–5)

REVIEWS: CL

Dodds, Dayle Ann. *The Shape of Things.* Illustrated by Julie Lacome. Cambridge, MA: Candlewick Press, 1994.

Basic shapes become houses, Ferris wheels, sailboats, and eggs when windows, lights, an ocean, and a mother hen are added to complete the transformations. By the end of the book, readers will be able to find many shapes of every kind. (Ages 3–5)

REVIEWS: HBG 03/01/95; SLJ 02/01/95; BL 01/15/95; CL

Ehlert, Lois. *Color Farm.* Illustrated by the author. New York: J. B. Lippincott, 1990.

Meticulously arranged die-cuts use geometric shapes to bring roosters, chickens, sheep, cows, and other farm animals to life. Readers will be captivated as brightly colored faces of animals transform as squares, hexagons, circles, diamonds, and hearts are added and removed. *Color Farm* is a handy book for teaching color, shape, and animal recognition. *Color Zoo* is another notable book of shapes by Ehlert. (Ages 2–5)

REVIEWS: HBG 09/01/97; HBG 03/01/91; BL 11/15/90; SLJ 11/01/90; PW 10/12/90; CL

Falwell, Cathryn. *Shape Space.* Illustrated by the author. New York: Clarion Books, 1992

When a young dancer discovers and opens a large red box filled with shapes, the activities and fun are unlimited. Falwell's book encourages movement through the exploration of various shapes. (Ages 4–5)

REVIEWS: HBG 03/01/93; HBM 01/01/93; BL 10/15/92; SLJ 10/01/92; PW 08/10/92; CL

Freymann, Saxton. *Food for Thought: The Complete Book of Concepts for Growing Minds.* New York: Arthur A. Levine Books, 2005.

Uniquely carved eggplants, leeks, strawberries, squashes, pineapples, and a multitude of other fruits and vegetables are used to teach shapes, colors, numbers, letters, and opposites. Readers will gleefully turn pages as fresh, entertaining food sculptures are presented. (Ages 1–4)

REVIEWS: HBG 10/01/05; SLJ 03/01/05; PW 02/28/05; BL 01/01/05; KR 12/15/04; CL

Guillain, Charlotte. *Comparing Shapes.* Chicago: Heinemann Library, 2009.

This book asks older preschoolers to draw circles, triangles, ovals, diamonds, and other common shapes. After drawing the shapes, they are challenged to spot them in photographs of drums, houses, stadiums, sheds, and windows. The back matter includes sections on comparing shapes, describing shapes, shapes to know, words to know, and a note to parents and teachers. (Ages 4–5)

Hello Kitty, Hello Shapes! Illustrated by Higashi Glaser. New York: Harry N. Abrams, 2005.

With the turn of each page, the lovable kitten Hello Kitty introduces shapes and illustrates how each is a part of her daily life. (Ages 1–5)

REVIEWS: PW 02/03/03

Hoban, Tana. *Round and Round and Round.* Photographed by the author. New York: Greenwillow Books, 1983.

Bold photographs of familiar animals, plants, and objects, including peas, logs, balloons, and tires, are used to introduce children to circles. (Ages 2–5)

REVIEWS: HBM 06/01/83; SLJ 04/01/83

Hoban, Tana. *Shapes, Shapes, Shapes.* Photographed by the author. New York: Greenwillow Books, 1986.

Bold photographs of familiar objects such as sailboats, barrels, tambourines, lunch boxes, and shoes are used to introduce children to multiple shapes. (Ages 2–5)

REVIEWS: CL

Lane, Penny Ann. *First Shapes in Buildings.* London: Frances Lincoln, 2010.

The Pantheon, St. Peter's Piazza, the Gherkin, Stonehenge, the entrance to the Louvre Museum, and other great architectural structures are used to demonstrate both simple and complex geometric shapes. (Ages 4–5)

REVIEWS: CL

Loughrey, Anita. *Circles.* Illustrated by Sue Hendra. Irvine, CA: QEB Publishing, 2010.

Loughrey's book is more than a simple introduction to circles—it teaches children to distinguish them from other shapes as well. In addition to identifying, counting, and drawing circles, preschoolers learn color and spatial concepts, and search for circles in locations familiar to them (the sandbox, the kitchen, the playground). Other notable titles in the QEB Shapes around Us series include *Rectangles*, *Squares*, and *Triangles*. (Ages 3–5)

REVIEWS: HBG 04/01/11; CL

MacCarthy, Patricia. *Ocean Parade: A Counting Book.* Illustrated by the author. New York: Dial Books for Young Readers, 1990.

In addition to counting from one to one hundred, this book introduces children to colors and shapes through encountering an array of fish and other ocean wonders. (Ages 3–5)

REVIEWS: HBG 09/01/90; SLJ 07/01/90; PW 02/23/90

MacDonald, Suse. *Shape by Shape.* Illustrated by the author. New York: Little Simon, 2009.

Carefully positioned die-cut circles, triangles, crescents, semicircles, ovals, and other shapes are presented one by one to create the eyes, teeth, mouth, and head of the biggest dinosaur ever—a Brachiosaurus. In addition to learning shapes, children will enjoy the suspense that grows until the last foldout page of the book is revealed. (Ages 3–5)

REVIEWS: PW 06/29/09; SLJ 06/01/09; BL 05/01/09; CL

Martin, Elena. *So Many Circles.* Bloomington, MN: Yellow Umbrella Books, 2006.

Dedicated solely to circles, Martin's book includes photographs of pancakes, traffic lights, flowers, the moon, and other circles found in nature and everyday life. (Ages 3–5)

McMillan, Bruce. *Fire Engine Shapes.* Photographed by the author. New York: Lothrop, Lee, & Shepard Books, 1988.

Using color photographs of a fire engine and an explorative four-year-old girl, this book introduces squares, rectangles, diamonds, hexagons, circles, and other traditional shapes. The back matter provides a definition of shapes and indexes the shapes shown in the book. (Ages 4–5)

REVIEWS: SLJ 10/01/88; BL 09/01/88

Micklethwait, Lucy. *I Spy Shapes in Art.* Devised and selected by the author. New York: Greenwillow Books, 2004.

Through the art of Winslow Homer, Henri Matisse, Georgia O'Keeffe, Andy Warhol, and other greats, readers are encouraged to search for rectangles, semicircles, ovals, diamonds, hearts, and more. Micklethwait's book is an ingenious way to introduce preschoolers to both art and shapes. (Ages 3–5)

REVIEWS: HBG 04/01/05; SLJ 09/01/04; PW 08/23/04; BL 08/01/04; KR 07/01/04; CL

Minden, Cecilia. *Shapes Everywhere.* Ann Arbor, MI: Cherry Lake Publishing, 2011.

Moving beyond basic shapes, this book introduces spheres, cubes, cones, and the concept of three-dimensional shapes. The back matter includes recommended books and websites, a glossary, a list of words from the book, and an index. (Ages 4–5)

Mitten, Luana K. *Three Dimensional Shapes: Cones.* Photographed by Only-Vectors et al. Vero Beach, FL: Rourke Publishing, 2009.

Once the author illustrates and explains the attributes of a cone in a manner older preschoolers can grasp (big circle, little point), they are shown two pictures. Only one of the two contains a cone, and readers are asked, "Which is a cone?" As the correct answer is revealed on the following page, arrows highlight the big circle and little point. In addition to an index, the back matter includes further readings and recommended websites. Other notable books in the Three Dimensional Shapes series include *Spheres, Cylinders,* and *Cubes.* (Ages 4–5)

Montague-Smith, Ann. *First Shape Book.* Illustrated by Mandy Stanley. Boston: Kingfisher Publications, 2002.

In addition to identifying basic shapes, children are encouraged to discuss, compare, and draw shapes. Questions such as "Can you draw a triangle?" "How many blue ovals can you see?" "Which circles do you like to eat?" and "Which shape has the most sides?" are included on each page. Front matter includes a detailed table of contents and suggestions for parents from the author. (Ages 4–5)

REVIEWS: SLJ 07/01/02; PW 05/06/02; CL

Nayer, Judy. *What's the Shape?* New York: Newbridge Educational Publishing, 1997.

This large-format book presents vivid photographs and familiar objects to help children recognize the many shapes around them. A sixteen-page teacher's guide filled with activities, educational strategies, and resources is also included. (Ages 3–5)

Olson, Nathan. *Stars around Town.* Photographed by Kelly Garvin. Mankato, MN: Capstone Press, 2007.

Simple text and brilliant photographs introduce readers to the various places that stars can be found in their community. Other notable books in the Shapes around Town series include *Circles around Town, Ovals around Town, Rectangles around Town, Squares around Town,* and *Triangles around Town.* (Ages 4–5)

REVIEWS: CL

Petty, Colin. *Shapes.* Illustrated by the author. Hauppauge, NY: Barron's Educational Series, 2006.

As children place a finger in a small hole and slide it to the left or right, the answer to the question "What shape?" appears in a cutout box on the corresponding page. As one of the four titles in the Concept Sliders series, *Shapes* is an entertaining way to introduce basic shapes to youngsters. (Ages 2–5)

REVIEWS: PW 08/28/06

Powers, Amelia. *Giant Pop-Out Shapes.* San Francisco: Chronicle Books, 2007.

Learning about circles, squares, triangles, ovals, stars, and hearts is easy when buttons, crackers, slices of pizza, and other everyday items are teaching aids. As pages unfold, revealing giant pop-out shapes, readers receive additional surprises. (Ages 1–4)

REVIEWS: SLJ 01/01/08; PW 08/27/07

Ranchetti, Sebastiano. *Shapes in Animals.* Illustrated by the author. Pleasantville, NY: Weekly Reader Books, 2008.

Brightly illustrated pages of circles, squares, triangles, spirals, and stars become eyes, scales, teeth, shells, and starfish. (Ages 2–4)

REVIEWS: CL

Rau, Dana Meachen. *Many-Sided Shapes.* New York: Marshall Cavendish Benchmark, 2007.

Photographs of signs, houses, kites, and other day-to-day items are used to teach children about circles, stars, diamonds, hexagons, pentagons, and more. (Ages 3–5)

REVIEWS: CL

Reidy, Hannah. *All Sorts of Shapes.* Illustrated by Emma Dodd. Minneapolis: Picture Window Books, 2005.

Picture frames, pizzas, cakes, bubbles, ices cubes, pastas, and fruits are used to introduce shapes, patterns, and spatial concepts. The back matter includes fun facts, words to know, and recommended books and websites. (Ages 3–5)

REVIEWS: SLJ 06/01/05; CL

Reiss, John J. *Shapes.* Illustrated by the author. Scarsdale, NY: Bradbury Press, 1974.

Animals introduce readers to brightly colored shapes and teach them how shapes can be used to make additional shapes (triangles to make pyramids, and circles to make spheres). (Ages 4–5)

REVIEWS: SLJ 12/01/74

Richards, Kitty. *Thumper's Shapes.* Illustrated by Lori Tyminski, Maria Elena Naggi, and Giorgio Vallorani. New York: Disney Enterprises, 2007.

Thumper and his sisters search for ovals, triangles, squares, and other basic shapes as they frolic through the forest. (Ages 3–5)

Rissman, Rebecca. *Shapes in Sports.* Illustrated by the author. Chicago: Heinemann Library, 2009.

Playing fields, checkered flags, sandpits, balls, and other sports-related objects teach children about rectangles, semicircles, diamonds, squares, and other shapes. Other titles in the Spot the Shape series include *Shapes in the Garden, Shapes in Building, Shapes in Art,* and *Shapes in Music.* (Ages 4–5)

REVIEWS: BL 09/01/09

Sarfatti, Esther. *Shapes: Rectangles.* Vero Beach, FL: Rourke Publishing, 2008.

Vibrant photographs of familiar objects like books, doors, swimming pools, and sandboxes prove that rectangles are everywhere. Other shape books in the series include *Shapes: Circles, Shapes: Squares,* and *Shapes: Triangles.* The back matter includes an index, recommended books for further reading, and recommended websites. (Ages 3–5)

Scarry, Richard. *Richard Scarry's Shapes and Opposites.* Illustrated by the author. New York: Sterling Publishing, 2008.

In addition to presenting triangles, squares, and circles, Scarry's book introduces spatial concepts like curved and straight; over, under, and around; up and down; clean and dirty; and more. (Ages 3–5)

Schachner, Judy. *Skippyjon Jones Shape Up.* Illustrated by the author. New York: Dutton Children's Books, 2008.

Skippyjon Jones, America's favorite Siamese kitty boy, stays in shape with shapes as he runs in circles, salsa dances on squares, reaches for stars, rocks back and forth on crescents, and balances diamonds. (Ages 3–5)

REVIEWS: CL

Shapes. New York: Scholastic, 2007.

As preschoolers identify and point to shapes on the left side of the book, they touch bumpy circles, smooth squares, scratchy triangles, and rough rectangles on the right. (Ages 0–2)

REVIEWS: CL

Shapes and Patterns. New York: PlayBac Publishing, 2007

Bananas, herons, thorns, cactus pads, chameleons, artichokes, and an abundance of additional gifts from nature illustrate both simple and complex shapes, patterns, and textures. Older preschoolers will be lured to the bold, colorful photographs. (Ages 4–5)

Shapiro, Arnold. *Triangles.* Illustrated by Bari Weissman. New York: Dial Books for Young Readers, 1992.

When readers turn each page of this three-sided book, triangles in the form of trees, tents, mountains, and sails are formed. Other books in the Dial Playshapes Book series include *Circles* and *Squares*. (Ages 0–5)

REVIEWS: HBG 09/01/92; PW 04/13/92; KR 01/15/92

Thong, Roseanne. *Round Is a Mooncake: A Book of Shapes.* Illustrated by Grace Lin. San Francisco: Chronicle Books, 2000.

Both shapes and Chinese American culture are taught as a young Chinese American girl explores her neighborhood for round, square, and rectangle items. The back matter highlights many of the book's items and customs, including dim sum, inking stones, and lucky money. (Ages 3–5)

REVIEWS: HBG 04/01/01; BL 12/01/00; PW 09/15/00; KR 09/01/00; SLJ 08/01/00

Walsh, Ellen Stoll. *Mouse Shapes.* Illustrated by the author. Orlando, FL: Harcourt, 2007.

While fleeing from a cat, three creative mice discover a pile of shapes and build houses, trees, wagons, books, and fish. They even craft three large scary mice to frighten the troublesome cat. (Ages 3–5)

REVIEWS: PW 07/23/07; SLJ 07/01/07; BL 07/01/07; HBM 07/01/07

Watt, Mélanie. *Shapes with Ocean Animals.* Illustrated by the author. Tonawanda, NY: Kids Can Press, 2005.

Triangle fish, square stingrays, circle puffer fish, oval crabs, and other marine animals come alive in this small book of shapes. (Ages 1–2)

REVIEWS: PW 04/25/05; CL

Weninger, Brigitte. *Zara Zebra Draws.* Illustrated by Anna Laura Cantone. New York: North-South Books, 2002.

As Zara draws lines, circles, triangles, rectangles, and squares, readers are challenged to imagine if they are worms, hoops, mountains, and other objects. When Zara puts all the shapes together as the story ends, she creates a house. (Ages 1–3)

REVIEWS: CL

Williams, Rozanne Lanczak. *I Have Shapes.* Illustrated by Pam Thompson. Huntington Beach, CA: Creative Teaching Press, 2002.

> This book encourages preschoolers to count their way through hearts, squares, rectangles, ovals, and other basic shapes. When all the shapes are combined, they form a colorful butterfly. The back matter includes a sight-word activity for early readers. (Ages 2–5)

Young, Laura. *Shapes at the Beach.* New York: Rosen Publishing Group, 2003.

> Beach balls, umbrellas, towels, sails, and ice-cream cones are used to teach triangles, circles, and squares. (Ages 2–4)

Spatial and Opposites

Crews, Donald. *Flying.* Illustrated by the author. New York: Greenwillow Books, 1986.

> Over, across, into, and down are a few of the spatial concepts explored in Crew's award-winning book. Preschoolers of all ages will find the smooth rhythm of the text and animated, airbrushed planes delightful. (Ages 0–5)
>
> REVIEWS: SLJ 10/01/86; BL 09/01/86

Curious George: Before and After. Boston: Houghton Mifflin, 2006.

> As readers turn pages and lift flaps, they will take an adventure with George as he experiences how it feels to be hungry and full, go up and down, and be dirty and clean. About more than simply opposites, this colorful and sophisticated book in rhyme also teaches sequence and consequences. (Ages 1–3)
>
> REVIEWS: CL

Freymann, Saxton. *Food for Thought: The Complete Book of Concepts for Growing Minds.* New York: Arthur A. Levine Books, 2005.

> Uniquely carved eggplants, leeks, strawberries, squashes, pineapples, and a multitude of other fruits and vegetables are used to teach shapes, colors, numbers, letters, and opposites. Readers will gleefully turn pages as fresh, entertaining food sculptures are presented. (Ages 1–4)
>
> REVIEWS: HBG 10/01/05; SLJ 03/01/05; PW 02/28/05; BL 01/01/05; CL

Heck, Ed. *Big Fish Little Fish.* Illustrated by the author. New York: Price Stern Sloan, 2007.

> With the use of simple text and bold, bright illustrations, youngsters explore several spatial concepts, such as big, little, front, above, inside, and fast, as an entertaining underwater adventure unfolds. (Ages 2–5)
>
> REVIEWS: PW 08/20/07

Hoban, Tana. *Exactly the Opposite.* Photographed by the author. New York: Greenwillow Books, 1990.

> With outdoor settings as the backdrop for this wordless book of luminous color photographs, Hoban's work illustrates spatial concepts like near and far, front and back, and above and below, in addition to opposites, by using objects and settings recognizable to most preschool children. Because each spectacular photograph tells a story, the person sharing this book should be prepared to engage in intriguing discussions with the child. (Ages 2–5)
>
> REVIEWS: HBG 03/01/91; SLJ 10/01/90; BL 09/01/90; PW 08/31/90; PW 08/13/90

Hoban, Tana. *Is It Larger? Is It Smaller?* Photographed by the author. New York: Greenwillow Books, 1985.

> Bold photographs of familiar objects, people, and animals, such as leaves, fish, boats, and snowmen, are used to introduce children to concepts of large and small. (Ages 2–5)
>
> REVIEWS: KR 03/15/85

Intriago, Patricia. *Dot.* Illustrated by the author. New York, Farrar, Straus, & Giroux, 2011.

> Through imaginative illustrations and simple rhymes, dots demonstrate simple concepts like stop and go, up and down, loud and quiet, happy and sad, soft and hard, and more. (Ages 3–5)
>
> REVIEWS: HBG 04/01/12; SLJ 08/01/11; PW 07/18/11; CL

Johnson, Tami. *Above and Below.* Photographed by Karon Dubke et al. Mankato, MN: Capstone Press, 2011.

> In both English and Spanish, the concepts of above and below are taught through vivid illustrations and simple, bilingual text. The back matter includes additional facts, a glossary, and websites related to the book.

Other notable titles in the Where Words series include *In and Out, Up and Down*, and *Near and Far*. (Ages 4–5)

REVIEWS: CL

Little, Patricia. *When This Box Is Full.* Illustrated by Donald Crews. New York: Greenwillow Books, 1993.

The narrator's wooden box may be empty in January, but as time passes, memorable belongings are added. By December, treasures like valentines, seashells, leaves, and wishbones have filled the empty space. In addition to learning spatial relationships, concepts such as months of the year, seasons, and colors are skillfully blended into this delightful book. (Ages 2–5)

REVIEWS: PW 01/21/97; HBG 03/01/94; SLJ 01/01/94; BL 12/01/93; PW 10/25/93; KR 10/15/93

MacDonald, Suse. *Look Whooo's Counting.* Illustrated by the author. New York: Scholastic, 2000.

Young Owl learns to count as she flies through the night sky and encounters animals on hills, in the grass, on trees, and among flowers. Children with advanced number recognition abilities will be in awe as they discover that the number representing each cut-paper animal is visually formed in the animal's body (e.g., the tails of the mice form the number two, the horns on the sheep resemble the number six). Counters of all ages will enjoy this imaginative book. (Ages 3–5)

REVIEWS: HBG 04/01/01; SLJ 12/01/00; PW 10/16/00; BL 10/15/00; KR 10/01/00; CL

Maestro, Betsy. *Traffic: A Book of Opposites.* Illustrated by Giulio Maestro. New York: Crown Publishers, 1981.

Readers learn the differences between over and under, stop and go, big and little, dark and light, and far and away as the little pink car in this story travels home. (Ages 1–4)

Mitten, Luana K. *Opposites: Open and Closed.* Photographed by Matthew Cole et al. Vero Beach, FL: Rourke Publishing, 2009.

Jaws, eyes, mouths, hands, arms, and other body parts and objects are used to explore the concepts of open and closed. The back matter recommends websites and additional books on the topic. Other notable books in the Opposites series include *Big and Small, Front and Back*, and *Hard and Soft*. (Ages 4–5)

Mitten, Luana K., and Meg Greve. *Around and Through.* Photographed by Nicole S. Young et al. Vero Beach, FL: Rourke Publishing, 2010.

Children enjoying a day at the park use gates, poles, tunnels, swings, and monkey bars to illustrate the spatial concepts around and through. The back matter includes recommended websites. Additional titles in the Location Words series include *In and Out*, *Near and Far*, and *Under and Over*. (Ages 4–5)

My First Look at Sizes. Photographed by Stephen Oliver. New York: Random House, 1990.

Photographs of familiar objects are used to illustrate size perception, including big and little; big to little; big, bigger, and biggest; tiny things; and things of the same size. (Ages 4–5)

My First Opposites Board Book. Photographed by Jane Burton et al. New York: DK Publishing, 2006.

Photographs of children, animals, and familiar objects are used to teach big and small, long and short, hot and cold, hard and soft, full and empty, and many more spatial concepts. (Ages 1–4)

REVIEWS: PW 04/28/03

Patricelli, Leslie. *Quiet Loud.* Illustrated by the author. Cambridge, MA: Candlewick Press, 2003.

Through simple text and bold, appealing illustrations, preschoolers learn the difference between quiet (whispering, thinking, and snow) and loud (screaming, singing, and rainstorms). Other notable spatial books by Patricelli include *Big Little* and *Yummy Yucky*. (Ages 1–3)

REVIEWS: PW 09/15/03; CL

Petty, Colin. *Opposites.* Illustrated by the author. Hauppauge, NY: Barron's Educational Series, 2006.

As children place a finger in a small hole and slide it to the left or right, they are introduced to spatial concepts including, big and small, tall and short, wet and dry, slow and fast, and inside and outside. *Opposites* is one of the four titles in the Concept Sliders series. (Ages 2–5)

REVIEWS: PW 08/28/06

Ransome, James E. *New Red Bike!* Illustrated by the author. New York: Holiday House, 2011.

> As Tom enjoys his new red bicycle with his friend Sam, preschoolers will learn concepts like up, down, around, under, behind, and across. (Ages 4–5)
>
> REVIEWS: HBG 10/01/11; SLJ 04/01/11; PW 01/17/11; CL

Reiser, Lynn. *Ten Puppies.* Illustrated by the author. New York: Greenwillow Books, 2003.

> With the aid of a dog and her adopted puppies, readers learn to count to ten in multiple ways. Each page categorizes puppies by unique traits, including tongues (pink or blue), ears (floppy or perky), tails (curly or straight), fur (shaggy or smooth), and paws (little or small), and youngsters are encouraged to count the number of puppies in each group. In the end, however, all ten share one common characteristic—they grow up to become dogs. (Ages 3–5)
>
> REVIEWS: HBG 10/01/03; PW 05/26/03; HBM 05/01/03; SLJ 04/01/03; KR 03/15/03; CL

Ring, Susan. *Big or Small?* Illustrated by Grant Woodrow et al. Bloomington, MN: Yellow Umbrella Books, 2006.

> Photographs of elephants, gorillas, horses, birds, fish, and giraffes teach readers the concepts of big and small. (Ages 3–5)

Scarry, Richard. *Richard Scarry's Shapes and Opposites.* Illustrated by the author. New York: Sterling Publishing, 2008.

> Scarry's book teaches basic shapes in addition to introducing spatial concepts like curved and straight; over, under, and around; up and down; and clean and dirty. (Ages 3–5)

Seeger, Laura Vaccaro. *First the Egg.* Illustrated by the author. New Milford, CT: Roaring Brook Press, 2007.

> Seeger uses small, subtle die-cuts and textured illustrations to demonstrate sequencing to preschool children. In addition to learning that chickens were once eggs, readers discover that frogs were once tadpoles, that flowers grow from seeds, and that even stories and pictures begin as words and paint. As this skillful story comes to a close, an age-old question resurfaces—which came first, the chicken or the egg? (Ages 3–5)
>
> REVIEWS: BL 02/01/08; HBM 11/01/07; SLJ 11/01/07; KR 09/01/07; PW 08/20/07; CL

CHAPTER 2

Wordless Picture Books

Wordless Picture Books

Wordless picture books tell a story through detailed illustrations without using words. Through picture books, preschoolers develop creativity skills as they use their imaginations; develop language and thinking skills; learn that stories have a beginning, middle, and end (sequencing skills); interpret stories in their own way; verbalize actions in their own words; learn to make judgments; discover cause and effect; strengthen eye coordination skills; and retell stories again and again.

Alborough, Jez. *Hug.* Illustrated by the author. Cambridge, MA: Candlewick Press, 2000.

> Walking through the jungle alone, a sad chimpanzee comes to tears as he sees elephants, snakes, lions, and other animals embracing lovingly. His sadness is replaced by joy, however, when his mother arrives and gives the chimp the tender hug he both desires and deserves. Rounds

of hugs are in store for all the animals as this tender story concludes. (Ages 2–5)

REVIEWS: PW 10/17/05; HBG 10/01/02; PW 12/03/01; HBG 04/01/01; SLJ 12/01/00; PW 11/20/00; KR 11/01/00

Andreasen, Dan. *The Treasure Bath.* Illustrated by the author. New York: Henry Holt, 2009.

What begins as a humdrum bath becomes an underwater adventure when a school of jubilant fish leaps from beneath the bubbles and leads a child on a thrilling journey filled with maps and buried treasures. Although the contents of the chest, an assortment of soaps and shampoos, slightly curbs his enthusiasm, the freshly baked slice of cake and glass of milk awaiting the boy once he is dry and dressed for bed make him smile with joy. (Ages 2–5)

REVIEWS: SLJ 08/01/09; PW 07/13/09; BL 06/01/09; CL

Berner, Rotraut Susanne. *In the Town All Year 'Round.* Illustrated by the author. San Francisco: Chronicle Books, 2008.

This oversize book chronicles the people and activity of a town over the course of four seasons. The detailed pictures and multiple story lines will have readers flipping pages back and forth time and time again. (Ages 2–5)

REVIEWS: SLJ 12/01/08; BL 11/15/08; PW 10/06/08

Blake, Quentin. *Clown.* Illustrated by the author. New York: Henry Holt, 1996.

A discarded clown frantically searches city streets for someone to rescue his fellow discarded pals from a curbside garbage can. After being photographed, tossed, and chased by a vicious dog, the clown meets a teenage girl who agrees to save his friends after the clown helps her finish her chores. (Ages 3–5)

REVIEWS: PW 08/31/98; HBG 09/01/96; HBM 07/01/96; SLJ 05/01/96; BL 04/15/96; PW 03/25/96; CL

Briggs, Raymond. *The Snowman.* Illustrated by the author. New York: Random House, 1978.

When a young boy goes to bed, he dreams that the snowman built earlier in the day comes alive. Both are fascinated by the twilight hours—the snowman is amazed by everyday items like televisions, flowers, clothes, dentures, and skateboards, and the young boy sets out on a flight around the city he will never forget. Another generation of preschoolers will enjoy telling this classic tale. (Ages 4–5)

REVIEWS: SLJ 04/01/11; BL 05/15/88; CL

Brown, Craig. *The Patchwork Farmer.* Illustrated by the author. New York: Greenwillow Books, 1989.

An accident-prone farmer must mend his overalls frequently, as he tears them again and again while conducting everyday chores. By the end of the story, his blue overalls become as colorful as the fields he tends. (Ages 3–5)

REVIEWS: HBG 03/01/90; BL 09/01/89

Burke, Tina. *Fly, Little Bird.* Illustrated by the author. La Jolla, CA: Kane/Miller Book Publishers, 2006.

A young girl and her puppy befriend a little bird who is unable to fly. Although the bird enjoys spending time with his newfound friends, he longs to be with his family. When he masters his flying techniques, he searches for, and is reunited with, his siblings. (Ages 3–5)

REVIEWS: HBG 10/01/06; BL 05/15/06; PW 02/20/06; CL

Carle, Eric. *Do You Want to Be My Friend?* Illustrated by the author. New York: Crowell, 1971.

A lonely gray mouse searches for a friend. As he eagerly chases the tails of horses, lions, monkeys, peacocks, and other contenders, he is unaware that his biggest predator is present throughout the book. *Do You Want to Be My Friend?* is a timeless book by one of children's literature's most beloved illustrators. (Ages 2–5)

REVIEWS: PW, 08/14/95; CL

Carmi, Giora. *A Circle of Friends.* Illustrated by the author. New York: Star Bright Books, 2003.

A circle of sharing is launched when a boy gives his muffin to a homeless man asleep on a park bench. After an astounding series of events, what began as an anonymous snack leads to a magnificent sunflower blooming outside the young boy's window. *A Circle of Friends* is an uplifting story that exemplifies the spirit of giving. (Ages 4–5)

REVIEWS: HBG 04/01/04; SLJ 01/01/04

Chesworth, Michael. *Rainy Day Dream.* Illustrated by the author. New York: Farrar, Strauss, & Giroux, 1992.

A strong gust of wind takes a young boy and his umbrella on a remarkable journey through forests, over lakes, above dams, beyond city high-rises, and across oceans. Soft watercolor illustrations bring the tale to a serene end as the youngster lands safely in the exact location where the adventure began. (Ages 3–5)

REVIEWS: HBG 03/01/93; BL 11/15/92; PW 11/09/92; SLJ 11/01/92; KR 10/01/92

Crews, Donald. *Truck.* Illustrated by the author. New York: Greenwillow Books, 1980.

As a truck travels from one loading dock to another, readers experience road signs, tunnels, truck stops, traffic jams, weather conditions, and more. (Ages 4–5)

REVIEWS: HBG 03/01/98; PW 03/22/91; PW 02/01/91; BL 05/15/88; CL

Crum, Shutta. *Mine!* Illustrated by Patrice Barton. New York: Alfred A. Knopf, 2011.

With the aid of the family dog and an assortment of toys, a toddler learns that sharing is much more fun than being selfish. *Mine!* is the ideal book for children who have not yet discovered the joy of generosity. (Ages 3–5)

REVIEWS: HBG 10/01/11; SLJ 06/01/11; PW 04/18/11; CL

Day, Alexandra. *Follow Carl!* Illustrated by the author. New York: Farrar, Straus, & Giroux, 1998.

A day of fun begins when a group of children asks Carl, a lovable rottweiler, to lead them in a game of follow the leader. As the characters stretch, climb walls, chase squirrels, roll in the grass, and finally take naps, young readers will be eager to participate in similar activities. (Ages 2–5)

REVIEWS: PW 09/29/98; BL 08/01/98; PW 06/29/98; KR 06/01/98; CL

dePaola, Tomie. *Pancakes for Breakfast.* Illustrated by the author. Orlando, FL: Harcourt, 1978.

A strong craving for a stack of pancakes serves as the driving force as an old lady encounters many obstacles before she is able to enjoy her breakfast. As the story concludes with an illustration of her sitting in a rocking chair close to a warm fire, the smile on her face assures readers that the reward was surely worth the effort. (Ages 3–5)

REVIEWS: PW 02/09/90; BL 05/15/88

Drescher, Henrik. *The Yellow Umbrella.* Illustrated by the author. New York: Bradbury Press, 1987.

A yellow umbrella and strong gust of wind take two zoo monkeys on an unforgettable adventure through the city, over mountains and oceans, and down rivers and waterfalls. The remarkable journey ends when a familiar river takes the mother and child back to their native habitat, where they are reunited with family and other loved ones. (Ages 2–5)

REVIEWS: SLJ 11/01/87; PW 06/26/87

Faller, Régis. *The Adventures of Polo.* Illustrated by the author. New Milford, CT: Roaring Brook Press, 2002.

Equipped with only a backpack and an umbrella, Polo begins an exciting journey consisting of rides on clouds, trips across oceans, underwater excursions, dinners on tropical islands, playing music with monkeys in their swank tree house, and befriending a lonely arctic snowman—all before returning home and relaxing in the shade of a lush tree. This seventy-five-page French import, combining full-page illustrations and small panels resembling graphic novels, is sure to heighten the imagination of preschoolers each time they read it. *Polo: The Runaway Book* is another notable wordless picture book featuring this lovable pup. (Ages 4–5)

REVIEWS: HBG 10/01/06; SLJ 06/01/06; PW 05/08/06; 05/01/06; KR 04/15/06; BL 03/15/06; CL

Gill, Madelaine. *The Spring Hat.* Illustrated by the author. New York: Simon & Schuster, 1993.

Mother Bunny's spring hat is lost and ruined when her three bunnies use it as a toy and accidently lose it in the stream. When the children of other mothers notice how hurt and angry she becomes, they gather flowers, cattails, leaves, and other decorative plants to make the most unique hat she has ever seen. Gill creates a springtime story that preschoolers will enjoy year-round. (Ages 3–5)

REVIEWS: HBG 09/01/93; SLJ 05/01/93; BL 03/01/93; BL 02/15/93; PW 12/28/92

Gutiérrez, Elisa. *Picturescape.* Illustrated by the author. Verona, NJ: Simply Read Books, 2005.

While a young boy visits an art museum, his imagination engulfs him. As he admires the works of art, he becomes one with the paintings and begins many magical adventures. (Ages 4–5)

REVIEWS: SLJ 02/01/06; CL

Henterly, Jamichael. *Good Night, Garden Gnome.* Illustrated by the author. New York: Dial Books for Young Readers, 2001.

Henterly's realistic watercolors reveal the magical world of gnomes. By day, gnomes simply stand in gardens and occasionally become toys for young children, but during the night, they become the true guardians of gardens, as they weed and water them, protect vegetables and young animals from predators, serve as companions to animals, and even return lost toys to children when necessary. This charming story offers an atypical perception of these often-ridiculed garden figurines. (Ages 3–5)

REVIEWS: HBG 10/01/01; SLJ 03/01/01; KR 01/01/01; CL

Himler, Ronald. *Dancing Boy.* Illustrated by the author. New York: Star Bright Books, 2005.

In the tradition of the Pied Piper, a naked blond child dances into a small rural town. As other children see him, they undress, join the dance, and follow the boy all around town. When they reach the edge of town, the blond visitor continues dancing down the dusty road while the children of the community return to their parents, slip back into their clothes, and return to their daily routines. After reading this book, children will want to take part in a spirited dance. (Ages 3–5)

REVIEWS: HBG 04/01/06; SLJ 09/01/05; CL

Hogrogian, Nonny. *Cool Cat.* Illustrated by the author. New York: Roaring Brook Press, 2009.

With the assistance of a case filled with art supplies and several devoted friends, Cool Cat transforms his bleak and littered world into one filled with beauty, color, and tranquillity. As young children turn the pages, they will encounter new animals and witness the creation of a new world. (Ages 3–5)

REVIEWS: SLJ 10/01/09; PW 08/24/09; KR 08/01/09; CL

Jay, Alison. *Welcome to the Zoo.* Illustrated by the author. New York: Dial Books for Young Readers, 2008.

The antics are endless when readers enter a zoo without cages—a place where there are no boundaries to prevent animals and humans from interacting freely. Children will eagerly follow the multiple subplots vividly depicted in Alison's signature crackle-varnish illustrations. What will be taken from, or added to, the blue-and-white picnic basket? Will the zookeeper ever catch the ostrich? What will the rambunctious poodle do next? Will the floating parrot balloon be captured? The back matter provides questions to further enhance this exploratory visit to the zoo. (Ages 3–5)

REVIEWS: BL 11/01/08; SLJ 11/01/08; PW 09/01/08

Keats, Ezra Jack. *Pssst! Doggie.* Illustrated by the author. New York: Franklin Watts, 1973.

When a cat invites a sleeping dog to dance, the two embark upon a magical dance that transports them through time and across the world. Traditional dances from Africa, Russia, Spain, France, and more are performed before the exhausted duo settles down for a much-deserved nap. (Ages 4–5)

Khing, T. T. *Where Is the Cake?* Illustrated by the author. New York: Abrams Books for Young Readers, 2007.

The adventure begins when two thieves run off with a freshly baked cake. On each panoramic page, more and more residents of the town enter the chase through meadows and woods, and over mountains and rivers. As with many wordless picture books for older preschoolers, several less prominent stories are just as exciting. Observant readers will enjoy the naughty antics of the monkeys, follow the snake as he slithers across the pages, trail the events of the soccer-playing frogs, track the mysterious and tall white plume, and more. Children who enjoy this book will be thrilled by the sequel, *Where Is the Cake Now?* (Ages 4–5)

REVIEWS: PW 04/16/07

Lee, Suzy. *Wave.* Illustrated by the author. San Francisco: Chronicle Books, 2008.

A young girl spends a day at the beach with her newfound playmates— five seagulls and the ocean. As she taunts and flirts with the tide, she experiences both the serenity and the intensity of waves before receiving delightful treasures from the sea. (Ages 3–5)

REVIEWS: PW 05/05/08; SLJ 05/01/08; KR 05/01/08; CL

Lehman, Barbara. *Rainstorm.* Illustrated by the author. Boston: Houghton Mifflin, 2007.

Life in a mansion can be lonely and boring on rainy days. Fortunately for the schoolboy living in this mansion, a memorable journey begins when he finds a key that opens a large trunk with downward steps. His journey down and up stairs, and through tunnels and doors, leads him to a lighthouse, where he befriends three children and a dog and experiences a fun-filled day. Thanks to the young boy's discovery, lonely days are behind him, rain or shine. (Ages 3–5)

REVIEWS: HBG 10/01/07; HBM 05/01/07; SLJ 03/01/07; PW 02/05/07; BL 01/01/07; CL

Lehman, Barbara. *The Red Book.* Illustrated by the author. Boston: Houghton Mifflin, 2004.

A young girl living in a major city finds a red book in the snow as she walks to school. A young boy on a small island on another continent finds a red book in the sand as he is walking on the beach. As the two read, something magical happens—they realize that the red books allow them to see each other. A desire to meet her new friend leads the girl on a journey to the small island. Imaginations will soar when reading this Caldecott Honor book. *Museum Tip* and *Trainstop* are additional notable wordless picture books by Barbara Lehman. (Ages 4–5)

REVIEWS: HBG 04/01/05; SLJ 11/01/04; BL 10/01/04; PW 09/13/04; HBM 09/01/04; CL

Maizlish, Lisa. *The Ring.* Photographed by the author. New York: Greenwillow Books, 1996.

When a bored youngster places a yellow plastic ring on his thumb, he becomes airborne and receives an unbelievable tour of New York City. With the aid of digitally enhanced photographs, readers are able to experience sights like the Empire State Building and the Statue of Liberty from the boy's perspective. (Ages 3–5)

REVIEWS: HBG 09/01/96; HBM 07/01/96; BL 06/01/96; PW 05/13/96; SLJ 05/01/96; KR 04/15/96; CL

McCully, Emily Arnold. *First Snow.* Illustrated by the author. New York: Harper & Row, 1985.

The mice are eager to participate in all of the winter activities associated with the first big snow of the season, especially sledding. Everyone except one small mouse in a pink scarf and pink toboggan—the idea of sledding terrifies her. After much persuasion from her family and friends, she finally sleds downhill, only to discover how fun and exhilarating sledding is. *First Snow* is sure to help little ones overcome their fears. (Ages 3–5)

REVIEWS: PW 09/30/88; SLJ 10/01/85; CL

Newman, Jeff. *The Boys.* Illustrated by the author. New York: Simon & Schuster Books for Young Readers, 2010.

Although he longs to play baseball with a group of boys in the park, the shy main character sits on a park bench with several elderly gentlemen. As the boy behaves and dresses more and more like the men each day, the four men become more youthful and help their new friend overcome his shyness. *The Boys* is an amusing book for highly developed preschoolers. (Ages 4–5)

REVIEWS: HBG 10/01/10; KR 02/15/10; PW 01/11/10; CL

Nyeu, Tao. *Wonder Bear.* Illustrated by the author. New York: Dial Books for Young Readers, 2008.

> When two children plant a hat seed in their garden, a large vine grows and produces a large white bear with a blue and orange hat. Readers will be astonished as monkeys, lion-shaped bubbles, flowers, and flying sea animals are all pulled from the magical hat. (Ages 3–5)
>
> REVIEWS: BL 09/15/08; SLJ 09/01/08; KR 08/15/08; PW 08/04/08; CL

Ormerod, Jan. *Moonlight.* Illustrated by the author. New York: Lothrop, Lee, & Shepard Books, 1982.

> A young girl's parents discover how difficult putting a toddler to bed can be. At times, baths, warm milk, and bedtime stories are not quite enough. Soothing illustrations make *Moonlight* an ideal bedtime story. (Ages 4–5)
>
> REVIEWS: BL 05/15/88; KR 09/01/82

Peddle, Daniel. *Snow Day.* Illustrated by the author. New York: Doubleday, 2000.

> Sparse watercolors chronicle the brief yet picturesque existence of a snowman. Children will enjoy retelling this simple and warm story from beginning to end. (Ages 3–5)
>
> REVIEWS: HBG 09/01/00; SLJ 03/01/00; BL 02/15/00; KR 12/15/99; PW 11/29/99

Pinkney, Jerry. *The Lion and the Mouse.* New York: Little, Brown Books for Young Readers, 2009.

> Using soft watercolors and colored pencils, Pinkney's Caldecott Medal–winning illustrations visually retell one of Aesop's most beloved fables, which teaches young readers that everyone can accomplish great things. (Ages 3–5)
>
> REVIEWS: HBG 11/01/09; SLJ 09/01/09; KR 08/01/09; BL 07/01/09; CL

Polhemus, Coleman. *The Crocodile Blues.* Illustrated by the author. Cambridge, MA: Candlewick Press, 2007.

> A simple trip to the grocery store for staples like milk, eggs, cereal, and birdseed becomes an unforgettable night for a man and his pet cockatoo when a humongous crocodile hatches from a refrigerated egg. The

jazzy feel of this comical story will engage the imaginations of older pre-schoolers. (Ages 4–5)

REVIEWS: SLJ 11/01/07; PW 09/24/07; KR 08/15/07; CL

Raschka, Chris. *A Ball for Daisy.* Illustrated by the author. New York: Schwartz & Wade Books, 2011.

Playful Daisy loves her red ball so much that she takes it everywhere she goes. She even sleeps with her beloved toy. One day at the park, a larger dog sees the ball, takes it away from Daisy, and plays too roughly with it. When Daisy's cherished ball pops, she is heartbroken. Luckily, the larger dog's owner is considerate enough to buy Daisy a new ball much like her old one, and she learns to love her new toy just as much. (Ages 3–7)

REVIEWS: HBG 04/01/12; HBM 09/01/11; SLJ 08/01/11; PW 06/13/11; CI

Rodriguez, Béatrice. *The Chicken Thief.* Illustrated by the author. New York: Enchanted Lion Books, 2010.

The chase begins as Fox steals Chicken from Bear's front yard. As Fox is pursued by Bear, Rooster, and Rabbit, it becomes apparent that Fox has no desire to harm Chicken—actually, the two are rather fond of each other. (Ages 4–5)

REVIEWS: SLJ 04/01/11; SLJ 08/01/10; BL 06/01/10; PW 04/19/10; CL

Savage, Stephen. *Where's Walrus?* Illustrated by the author. New York: Scholastic Press, 2011.

No one ever imagined that Walrus was the king of disguise, until he escaped from the zoo. He assimilates quite well as a fountain statue, a mannequin, a fireman, a can-can dancer, and more. Children will amus-ingly join the zookeeper as he dashes around town in search of Walrus. (Ages 3–5)

REVIEWS: HBG 10/01/11; HBM 03/01/11; PW 02/14/11; SLJ 02/01/11; KR 01/15/11; CL

Schories, Pat. *Jack and the Missing Piece.* Illustrated by the author. Asheville, NC: Front Street, 2004.

Given that Jack, a spirited orange and white terrier, continuously knocks down the tower of blocks that two young boys are constructing, he is the obvious suspect when the crowning tower piece cannot be found.

The simple but exhilarating mystery unfolds when the boys realize that Jack has been falsely accused. Preschoolers of many ages will enjoy this uncomplicated whodunit. Other noteworthy wordless picture books by Schories featuring Jack include *Breakfast for Jack*, *Jack Wants a Snack*, and *When Jack Goes Out*. (Ages 2–5)

REVIEWS: HBG 04/01/05; HBM 01/01/05; PW 12/20/04; SLJ 11/01/04; CL

Schories, Pat. *Mouse Around.* Illustrated by the author. New York: Farrar, Straus, & Giroux, 1991.

A baby mouse's fall from his nest into the back pocket of a plumber sets off what becomes a thrilling journey. As he travels from a box of doughnuts to a boy's paper route, a bakery, an automobile repair shop, a department store, an afternoon tea, and eventually back home to his warm nest with his family, readers will enjoy searching each page in detail for the valiant mouse as he survives each segment of the adventure. (Ages 3–5)

REVIEWS: HBG 09/01/91; SLJ 08/01/91; BL 06/15/91; KR 06/01/91; PW 05/24/91

Sís, Peter. *Dinosaur!* Illustrated by the author. New York: Greenwillow Books, 2000.

A young boy's imagination soars as a simple bath with a toy dinosaur turns into a prehistoric adventure with more than a dozen dinosaurs. Avid dinosaur fans will enjoy identifying the various species as they magically materialize from the tub. Front and back matter include names and illustrations of the dinosaurs featured in the book. (Ages 3–5)

REVIEWS: HBG 09/01/00; HBM 07/01/00; SLJ 06/01/00; BL 03/15/00; CL

Sís, Peter. *Ship Ahoy!* Illustrated by the author. New York: Greenwillow Books, 1999.

As a little boy sits in his living room, the couch transforms into a raft, canoe, pirate ship, submarine, and other vessels before the adventure ends. The simple yet enticing format of this book teaches preschoolers the clear difference between reality and fantasy. (Ages 3–5)

REVIEWS: SLJ 09/01/00; HBG 04/01/00; BL 09/01/99; HBM 08/01/99; KR 08/01/99; PW 07/19/99; CL

Slater, David Michael. *The Bored Book.* Illustrated by Doug Keith. Verona, NJ: Simply Read Books, 2009.

> When the grandfather of two restless siblings leads them to a book titled *The Bored Book*, the brother-and-sister team embarks on a journey filled with monsters, pirates, sea creatures, ancient worlds, and more—a journey that can be found only between the covers of books. This tale reveals the power and fascination of reading to older preschoolers. (Age 5)
>
> REVIEWS: SLJ 10/01/09

Spier, Peter. *Noah's Ark.* Illustrated by the author. New York: Dell Dragonfly Books, 2002.

> Through detailed illustrations and limited text, Spier retells one of the Bible's most beloved children's stories. The Caldecott Medal–winning book opens with the English translation of the Dutch poem "The Flood," by Jacobus Revius. (Ages 4–5)
>
> REVIEWS: SLJ, 04/01/11; PW 09/07/92; BL 05/15/88

Tafuri, Nancy. *Junglewalk.* Illustrated by the author. New York: Greenwillow Books, 1988.

> After reading a bedtime book titled *Jungles of the World*, a young boy dreams that his backyard becomes a jungle filled with tigers, toucans, gorillas, elephants, and other jungle animals and plants. This book is sure to encourage youngsters to explore their backyards, neighborhoods, parks, forests, and beyond. (Ages 2–5)
>
> REVIEWS: BL 03/01/88

Thomson, Bill. *Chalk.* Illustrated by the author. Tarrytown, NY: Marshall Cavendish, 2010.

> A rainy day, a bag of sidewalk chalk, and three children with vibrant imaginations are all it takes to turn a murky, run-of-the-mill day into an adventure guaranteed to captivate readers. Thomson's photorealistic acrylic-and-pencil illustrations are simply captivating. (Ages 4–5)
>
> REVIEWS: SLJ 04/01/11; HBG 10/01/10; SLJ 04/01/10; PW 01/25/10; CL

Tolman, Marije, and Ronald Tolman. *The Tree House.* Illustrated by the authors. Honesdale, PA: Lemniscaat, 2010.

> While reading and enjoying a quiet picnic in their intricate tree house, Brown Bear and Polar Bear receive visits from a variety of friends. As they welcome flamingos, a rhinoceros, pandas, owls, peacocks, and other animals, the tree house overflows with amusement and activity. When their guests bid them good-bye, the bears return to their tranquil lifestyle of reading, catching snowflakes, and enjoying cloud-filled days and moonlit nights. Children's imaginations will soar as they interpret the dreamlike illustrations of this oversize book. (Ages 3–5)
>
> REVIEWS: HBG 10/01/10; SLJ 04/01/10; PW 03/22/10; CL

Van Ommen, Sylvia. *The Surprise.* Illustrated by the author. Asheville, NC: Front Street, 2003.

> The mystery begins on the opening page as Sheep weighs herself on a scale. As she purchases dye from the fleece store, dyes her wool red, shaves herself, has the wool spun into yarn, and stays up late knitting, children realize that she is making a garment. But what is Sheep making, and whom is she making it for? The secret is revealed on the last page of this tender story, filled with perfectly sequenced gouache illustrations. (Ages 2–5)
>
> REVIEWS: HBG 10/01/07; BL 05/15/07; PW 05/14/07; SLJ 05/01/07; CL

Varon, Sara. *Chicken and Cat.* Illustrated by the author. New York: Scholastic Press, 2006.

> Cat is enjoying visiting his friend Chicken in New York City. Biking to the park and visits to Coney Island are great, but the drabness of apartment living makes Cat sad and homesick. Chicken has the ideal solution—he plants a rooftop garden that both of them can nurture and enjoy. *Chicken and Cat Clean Up* is another notable wordless picture book by Sara Varon. (Ages 4–5)
>
> REVIEWS: HBG 10/01/06; SLJ 05/01/06; HBM 03/01/06; BL 02/01/06; PW 01/30/06; CL

Vincent, Gabrielle. *Breakfast Time, Ernest and Celestine.* Illustrated by the author. New York: Greenwillow Books, 1982.

> Celestine is too sleepy to have breakfast and accidently breaks the bowl as she pushes the cereal away. She proves to Ernest that she is genu-

inely sorry by cleaning up the mess and eating a fresh bowl of cereal, as a polite little mouse should. (Ages 4–5)

REVIEWS: BL 05/15/88; SLJ 11/01/85

Vincent, Gabrielle. *A Day, a Dog.* Illustrated by the author. Asheville, NC: Front Street, 1999.

Minimalist charcoal sketches chronicle the journey of a fearless dog from the moment he is thrown from a car and abandoned to when he encounters an individual who is alone as well. The book addresses the horror of animal cruelty in a sophisticated and heartwarming fashion. (Ages 4–5)

REVIEWS: HBG 09/01/00; BL 07/27/00; SLJ 06/01/00; HBM 05/01/00; CL

Wiesner, David. *Tuesday.* Illustrated by the author. New York: Clarion Books, 1991.

At around 8 p.m. on Tuesday evening, lily pads rise and take frogs on a magical adventure. As the illustrations reveal the unforgettable events of the night, readers can only imagine what adventure the following Tuesday will bring. (Ages 4–5)

REVIEWS: PW 07/28/97; HBG 09/01/91; SLJ 05/01/91; BL 05/01/91; PW 03/01/91

Wilson, April. *April Wilson's Magpie Magic: A Tale of Colorful Mischief.* Illustrated by the author. New York: Dial Books for Young Readers, 1999.

Havoc commences when a young artist's magpie comes to life and flies off the paper. As colored pencils are used to create ripe red cherries, to entice the escaped bird back to the paper, chaos continues as the magpie bursts a bright orange balloon, starts a fire, and floods the paper with puddles, to name just a few of his antics. Even a locked cage and the artist's attempt to erase the rascally bird are unable to prevent additional mayhem. The whimsical detailed illustrations of Wilson's book will make this an instantaneous favorite. (Ages 3–5)

REVIEWS: HBG 09/01/99; BL 04/15/99; PW 04/05/99; SLJ 04/01/99; HBM 03/01/99; KR 02/01/99; CL

Yum, Hyewon. *Last Night.* Illustrated by the author. New York: Farrar, Straus, & Giroux, 2008.

When an angry young girl finally drifts asleep, her teddy bear comes alive and takes her on a moonlit journey through the woods, where she meets and frolics with foxes and lions. When morning comes, she not only finds herself back in her bed with her teddy bear but also realizes how much she loves her mother. Yum's linocut illustrations make this a unique read. (Ages 3–5)

REVIEWS: BL 11/15/08; PW 09/01/08; SLJ 09/01/08; CL

CHAPTER 3

Rhyming Books

Key to Review Sources

BL *Booklist;* **CL** *Children's Literature* (reviews searchable in *Children's Literature Comprehensive Database*); **HBG** *Horn Book Guide;* **HBM** *Horn Book Magazine;* **KR** *Kirkus Reviews;* **LJ** *Library Journal;* **PW** *Publisher's Weekly;* **SLJ** *School Library Journal;* **WLB** *Wilson Library Bulletin*

Some book reviews predate the edition of books because reviews refer to earlier editions.

Rhyming Books

Children learn language and strengthen their sense of rhythm by hearing the repetition of identical sounds in words found in these books. Additionally, rhyming books help preschoolers develop phonemic awareness, or the ability to segment sounds in spoken word.

Baker, Keith. *Little Green.* Illustrated by the author. New York: Red Wagon Books, 2005.

> A young boy paints the flight of a green hummingbird zipping, jigging, jagging, dipping, sipping, dashing, darting, zigging, and zagging outside his window. Baker combines a calming garden view and simple, lively rhyming text to create a gratifying story. (Ages 2–5)
>
> REVIEWS: PW 02/28/05; HBG 10/01/01; BL 04/15/01; SLJ 04/01/01; KR 03/01/01; PW 02/12/01; CL

Baker, Keith. *LMNO Peas.* Illustrated by the author. New York: Beach Lane Books, 2010.

> Delightful green peas announce and demonstrate their occupations as they romp through the pages of this rhyming alphabet book. As hundreds of builders, circus clowns, kayakers, quarterbacks, readers, and yogis weave through four-inch-high, brightly colored letters, youngsters will delight in the activities of these energized peas. (Ages 3–7)
>
> REVIEWS: PW 03/22/10; SLJ 03/01/10; KR 03/01/10; CL

Baker, Keith. *Potato Joe.* Illustrated by the author. Orlando, FL: Harcourt, 2008.

> As Potato Joe begins the count, ten lively potatoes count from one to ten and back again. As they play tic-tac-toe, get frightened by a huge black crow, get covered in snow, and swing their partner and do-si-do, they are joined by two garden friends, Tomato Flo and Watermelon Moe, before they return safely to the rich brown dirt for a snooze. The catchy text, based on the familiar nursery rhyme "One Potato, Two Potato," will quickly become a read-aloud favorite. (Ages 3–5)
>
> REVIEWS: PW 06/16/08; SLJ 06/01/08; KR 05/01/08; CL

Bang, Molly. *Ten, Nine, Eight.* Illustrated by the author. New York: Tupelo Books, 1996.

> The reader counts from ten to one as a father prepares his daughter for bed. The award-winning illustrations depict the warmth of a child's room (soft toys, snow falling through open windowpanes, and a mobile made of beautiful shells) and the wonder of love shared between a father and daughter. This book is sure to be a bedtime favorite. (Ages 2–4)
>
> REVIEWS: BL 11/15/98; PW 05/03/91; BL 12/15/89; CL

Bateman, Donna M. *Deep in the Swamp.* Illustrated by Brian Lies. Watertown, MA: Charlesbridge, 2007.

> While counting the young of mother river otters, snapping turtles, blue herons, rat snakes, crayfish, and more, children learn about the sounds, plants, and animals of the Okefenokee Swamp. The "Swamp Flora and Fauna Facts" section at the back of the book provides pictures and additional details. (Ages 3–5)
>
> REVIEWS: HBG 10/01/07; BL 05/15/07; SLJ 03/01/07; PW 01/15/07; KR 01/01/07; CL

Beaumont, Karen. *Duck, Duck Goose! (A Coyote's on the Loose!).* Illustrated by Jose Aruego and Ariane Dewey. New York: Harper Collins Publishers, 2004.

Follow the adventure as a group of frightened farm animals flee from what they believe is a hungry coyote on the loose. Expressive illustrations, suspense, and simple and flowing rhymes make this an amusing read-aloud. (Ages 3–5)

REVIEWS: HBG 10/01/04; BL 03/01/04; LJ 02/15/04; SLJ 02/01/04; CL

Bently, Peter. *King Jack and the Dragon.* Illustrated by Helen Oxenbury. New York: Dial Books for Young Readers, 2011.

Imaginations run rampant as three boys use cardboard boxes, sheets, sticks, trash bags, broken bricks, and quilts to build a castle. After building such a fine fortress, King Jack and his two brave knights spend all day protecting the castle from dragons and beasts. When the sun begins to set and giants (aka parents) take his knights home for the evening, King Jack must defend his castle all alone on a moonlit night. (Ages 3–5)

REVIEWS: HBG 04/01/12; SLJ 09/01/11; PW 05/16/11

Brown, Margaret Wise. *Sleepy ABC.* Illustrated by Karen Katz. New York: Harper Collins Publishers, 2010.

As four multicultural families prepare their toddlers for bedtime, readers will enjoy the rhymes accompanying each letter of the alphabet. Bold, bright, and simple illustrations will delight readers as they experience dreams and dark winds, feet that won't fall asleep, dark and starry nights, quiet that is all around, and finally, children who are fast asleep. (Ages 2–5)

REVIEWS: HBG 10/01/10; CL

Burleigh, Robert. *Messenger, Messenger.* Illustrated by Barry Root. New York: Atheneum Books for Young Readers, 2000.

Readers will enjoy spending a hectic and busy day with bicycle messenger Calvin Curbhopper as he makes deliveries. Although it is a cold day in the city, Calvin must travel over bridges, through revolving doors, and up escalators; wait in traffic; and deliver a package to the ninety-fifth floor of a high-rise building before his day ends and he can return to his warm apartment. (Ages 4–5)

REVIEWS: HBG 09/01/00; PW 06/19/00; SLJ 06/01/00; BL 05/15/00; CL

Capucilli, Alyssa Satin. *Mrs. McTats and Her Houseful of Cats.* Illustrated by Joan Rankin. New York: Margaret K. McElderry Books, 2001.

> Mrs. McTats and Abner, her loving cat, are quite happy living together in their country cottage. Daily scratches on the front door soon provide Mrs. McTats with twenty-five cats, including Basil, Jezebel, Rosebud, and Yodel. The twenty-sixth and final visitor is rather unique but absolutely completes the host of animals residing in the cottage. Both children and adults will appreciate the comical illustrations found in this book of rhymes, letters, and numbers. (Ages 3–5)
>
> REVIEWS: PW 05/24/04; BL 10/01/01; HBG 10/01/01; SLJ 08/01/01; PW 05/28/01; KR 05/01/01; CL

Cartwright, Reg. *What We Do.* Illustrated by the author. New York: Henry Holt, 2004.

> Bold, colorful illustrations and simple rhyming text describe how worms, monkeys, mice, pigs, and snakes wiggle, swing, scurry, guzzle, and slide. *What We Do* is an ideal story to encourage young children to get up and move. (Ages 2–5)
>
> REVIEWS: HBG 01/01/06; SLJ 10/01/05; PW 08/08/05; CL

Charles, N. N. *What Am I? Looking Through Shapes at Apples and Grapes.* Illustrated by Leo Dillon and Diane Dillon. New York: Blue Sky Press, 1994.

> Die-cuts and rhyming questions teach preschoolers colors, shapes, and fruits. Readers are sure to be astounded as they turn each striking page. (Ages 3–5)
>
> REVIEWS: HBG 03/01/95; SLJ 01/01/95; BL 11/15/94; PW 08/08/94; CL

Cline-Ransome, Lesa. *Quilt Alphabet.* Illustrated by James E. Ransome. New York: Holiday House, 2001.

> Using rural America as its backdrop, a picture and poem present clues to the object, plant, or animal chosen to represent each framed, quilted letter. Older preschoolers will enjoy solving the riddles, which range from the very obvious to the slightly abstract. As a convenience to the reader, answers are printed in the back of the book. (Ages 2–5)
>
> REVIEWS: HBG 04/01/02; SLJ 11/01/01; BL 10/01/01; PW 09/17/01; KR 08/01/01; CL

Cronin, Doreen. *Click, Clack, Splish, Splash: A Counting Adventure.* Illustrated by Betsy Lewin. New York: Atheneum Books for Young Readers, 2006.

> When a farmer falls asleep on the sofa, his animals embark on a unique fishing adventure. In this story in rhyme, children will enjoy the delightful expressions on the faces of the duck, chickens, cows, fish, and other creatures, as they learn to count from one to ten and from ten to one. (Ages 2–5)
>
> REVIEWS: HBG 10/01/06; KR 01/01/06; BL 01/01/06; SLJ 01/01/06; PW 11/21/05; CL

Cronin, Doreen. *Wiggle.* Illustrated by Scott Menchin. New York: Atheneum Books for Young Readers, 2005

> From sunrise to sunset, the energetic dog in Cronin's book demonstrates many ways to wiggle. As readers join in and wiggle with their shadows, toys, or maybe even in their underwear, they are sure to get all their wiggles out before it is time to say goodnight. (Ages 1–4)
>
> REVIEWS: HBG 10/01/05; HBM 09/01/05; SLJ 06/01/05; PW 05/23/05; BL 05/01/05; CL

Cummings, Pat. *My Aunt Came Back.* Illustrated by the author. New York: HarperFestival, 1998.

> Each time a young girl's aunt returns from an exotic location, she brings her niece memorable gifts like wooden shoes, quilted vests, painted fans, parasols, rings of gold, and berets. Before visiting Kathmandu, the aunt gives her niece a gift she will always cherish—a chance to travel to Kathmandu with her. Toddlers will enjoy repeating the rhyming words and sounds. (Ages 2–5)
>
> REVIEWS: SLJ 10/01/98; HBG 09/01/98; CL

Curious George: Before and After. Boston: Houghton Mifflin, 2006.

> As readers turn pages and lift flaps, they will take an adventure with George as he experiences how it feels to be hungry and full, go up and down, and be dirty and clean. About more than simply opposites, this colorful and sophisticated book in rhyme also teaches sequence and consequences. (Ages 1–3)
>
> REVIEWS: CL

Demarest, Chris L. *Firefighters A to Z.* Illustrated by the author. New York: Margaret K. McElderry Books, 2000.

> Action-filled pastel illustrations and simple, powerful rhymes demonstrate what occurs when a firefighter receives an emergency call. Written by a volunteer firefighter, this educational alphabet book emphasizes the dangers associated with fires and the importance of firefighters. *Firefighters A to Z* is also an appropriate title for observing National Fire Prevention Month in October. (Ages 2–5)
>
> REVIEWS: HBG 04/01/01; SLJ 12/01/00 BL 07/27/00; HBM 07/01/00; CL

Ehlert, Lois. *Fish Eyes: A Book You Can Count On.* Illustrated by the author. New York: Red Wagon Books, 1990.

> After imagining being a fish, children are taken on an underwater journey, where they see and count a variety of brightly colored fish. Ehlert's rhyming counting book will amuse early counters. (Ages 3–5)
>
> REVIEWS: PW 06/15/92; HBG 09/01/90; SLJ 05/01/90; PW 04/13/90; BL 03/01/90; CL

Elya, Susan Middleton, and Merry Banks. *N Is For Navidad.* Illustrated by Joe Cepeda. San Francisco: Chronicle Books, 2007.

> The Christmas season is celebrated in the tradition of may Latino families as *ángeles* are hung high, sweet *dulces* are prepared, a *nacimiento* is made, and *zapatos* are placed outside. Author notes provide additional information relating to Latino symbols and customs, including pronunciations and definitions for the Spanish words introduced. *N Is for Navidad* is an enlightening cultural experience for non-Latino readers. (Ages 3–5)
>
> REVIEWS: BL 11/01/07; KR 11/01/07; SLJ 10/01/07; CL

Ernst, Lisa Campbell. *This Is the Van That Dad Cleaned.* Illustrated by the author. New York: Simon & Schuster Books for Young Readers, 2005.

> In this cumulative tale, Dad's sparkling clean van loses its luster as toys, french fries, ketchup, baseball gloves, backpacks, candy corn, and a stuffed moose create one messy mishap after another. The charming tale ends with the children diligently cleaning the van for their father. (Ages 3–5)
>
> REVIEWS: HBG 10/01/05; HBM 05/01/05; SLJ 05/01/05; BL 04/01/05; CL

Falwell, Cathryn. *Turtle Splash! Countdown at the Pond.* Illustrated by the author. New York: Greenwillow Books, 2001.

> Ten turtles are startled by the bullfrogs, deer, butterflies, and mosquitoes they encounter as they lounge on a log at the pond. In addition to counting from ten to one, preschoolers will discover animals living in ponds and woodlands. The back matter includes detailed information relating to the animals appearing in the book and instructions for making leaf prints. (Ages 3–5)
>
> REVIEWS: HBG 04/01/02; SLJ 09/01/01; BL 08/01/01; PW 07/09/01; KR 07/01/01; CL

Fleming, Candace. *Oh, No!* Illustrated by Eric Rohmann. New York: Schwartz & Wade Books, 2012.

> While fleeing from a hungry tiger, Frog falls into a deep hole. One by one, his friends Mouse, Loris, Sun Bear, and Monkey try to save him, but they all become trapped in the hole as well. As Tiger peers down into the hole and drools in anticipation of a tasty feast, Elephant comes to the rescue. Preschoolers will enjoy the rhymes, repetition, and nonsense words like *ribbit-oops, pippa-eeek, wheee-haaaa,* and *ba-boom* as they turn the pages of this suspenseful tale. (Ages 3–5)
>
> REVIEWS: HBG 04/01/13; KR 08/01/12; SLJ 08/01/12; PW 07/09/12; KR 05/15/12; CL

Fleming, Denise. *In the Small, Small Pond.* Illustrated by the author. New York: Henry Holt, 1993.

> An energetic frog hops into a small pond and swims with tadpoles, geese, dragonflies, turtles, herons, and other inhabitants. The springy rhymes and dazzling images are the perfect introduction for children who are planning a visit to a pond. (Ages 2–5)
>
> REVIEWS: PW 10/19/98; HBG 03/01/94; BL 09/01/93; KR 08/15/93; PW 07/05/93; CL

Fox, Mem. *Ten Little Fingers and Ten Little Toes.* Illustrated by Helen Oxenbury. Orlando, FL: Harcourt, 2008.

> Babies from around the world unite in this book to share their commonalities—ten little fingers and ten little toes. Simple rhyming text, expressive pencil-and-watercolor illustrations, and an array of adorable toddlers make this a memorable lap book. (Ages 0–3)
>
> REVIEWS: HBM 01/01/09; SLJ 12/01/08; BL 11/15/08; 09/15/08; CL

Frazee, Marla. *Hush, Little Baby: A Folk Song with Pictures.* Illustrated by the author. Orlando, FL: Red Wagon Books, 2007.

In this story based on the well-known lullaby, an older sibling encourages her parents and others to soothe the wailing baby with a mockingbird, diamond ring, billy goat, and horse and cart. Amazingly, the baby stops bawling when the horse and cart tumble down a hill, and the baby returns to being "the sweetest little baby in town." Filled with expressive illustrations, *Horn Book Magazine* calls this "the sweetest— and definitely savviest—little version of this particular lullaby to date." (Ages 0–3)

REVIEWS: PW 04/16/07; PW 09/08/03; HBG 04/01/00; HBM 12/01/99; LJ 12/01/99; BL 11/15/99; SLJ 10/01/99; PW 08/30/99; KR 08/15/99; CL

Hayes, Sarah. *Nine Ducks Nine.* Illustrated by the author. New York: Lothrop, Lee, & Shepard Books, 1990.

Nine watchful ducks realize that a wily fox is trailing them as they enjoy a walk on a sunny day. One by one, the shrewd ducks break away, leading the fox down to the rickety bridge. Pastoral watercolors and humorous speech balloons add further appeal to this amusing, rhyming counting book. (Ages 3–5)

REVIEWS: PW 02/19/96; HBG 03/01/91; SLJ 12/01/90; PW 10/12/90; PW 10/2/90; CL

Hubbard, Patricia. *My Crayons Talk.* Illustrated by G. Brian Karas. New York: Henry Holt, 1996.

As a young girl's box of crayons talk, "Yackity. Clackity. Talk. Talk. Talk," purple shouts for bubble gum, blue calls the sky, gold brags, and red roars. Listeners will enjoy chanting along with the short rhythmic rhymes of this book prior to opening a box of crayons and creating their own pictures. (Ages 2–4)

REVIEWS: PW 05/24/99; HBG 09/01/96; SLJ; 05/01/96; BL 04/01/96; KR 03/01/96; CL

Hubbell, Patricia. *Wrapping Paper Romp.* Illustrated by Jennifer Plecas. New York: HarperFestival, 1998.

As a toddler unwraps a present, readers quickly realize that a creative mind and brightly colored wrapping paper and tissue paper can be just as much fun as the actual gift. Children age one and older will find the smooth rhyming couplets and joyous illustrations between the covers of this book delightful. (Ages 1–5)

REVIEWS: SLJ 02/01/99; CL

Intriago, Patricia. *Dot.* Illustrated by the author. New York: Farrar, Straus, & Giroux, 2011.

Dots demonstrate how versatile they can be—fast, sad, yummy, soft, shy, bouncing, making sounds, and more. Children will enjoy the imaginative illustrations and simple rhymes. (Ages 3–5)

REVIEWS: HBG 04/01/12; SLJ 08/01/11; PW 07/18/11; CL

Koller, Jackie French. *One Monkey Too Many.* Illustrated by Lynn Munsinger. Orlando, FL: Voyager Books, 2003.

Mayhem develops as mischievous monkeys encounter bicycles, golf carts, canoes, restaurants, hotels, and books. (Ages 3–5)

REVIEWS: PW 08/18/03; HBG 09/01/99; SLJ 05/01/99; PW 04/19/99; BL 04/15/99; HBM 03/01/99; CL

Krebs, Laurie. *We All Went on Safari: A Counting Journey through Tanzania.* Illustrated by Julia Cairns. Cambridge, MA: Barefoot Books, 2003.

Readers will count animals in both English and Swahili as they join a group of Maasai children walking through the grasslands, lakes, and rocky hillside glens of Tanzania. Back pages include detailed information of Tanzania, the Maasai people, Swahili names, and counting in Swahili. (Ages 3–5)

REVIEWS: HBG 10/01/03; SLJ 04/01/03; PW 03/24/03; CL

Laden, Nina. *Peek-a-Who?* Illustrated by the author. San Francisco: Chronicle Books, 2000.

Simple rhyming text and die-cut windows make this the ideal guessing book for preschool children. The mirrored end page, appropriated captioned, "Peek a YOU!" is sure to delight young readers again and again. (Ages 0–2)

REVIEWS: SLJ 07/01/00

Leuck, Laura. *One Witch.* Illustrated by S. D. Schindler. New York: Walker & Company, 2003.

Realizing that her cauldron is empty, a witch borrows enough ingredients from her friends to make a gruesome brew. As children count from one to ten, then back to one, they will enjoy meeting cats, goblins, skeletons, and other bizarre creatures invited to feast with the gracious witch. *One Witch* is an eerie yet amusing Halloween story. (Ages 3–5)

REVIEWS: HBG 04/01/04; BL 09/01/03; PW 08/04/03; SLJ 08/01/03; CL

Lewis, Kevin. *Chugga-Chugga Choo-Choo.* Illustrated by Daniel Kirk. New York: Hyperion Books for Children, 1999.

From sunup until bedtime, children will enjoy riding this steam engine as it journeys through the country, around mountains, into tunnels, and across rivers to deliver a freight of toys to the city. Preschoolers are sure to make train sounds while reading the book. (Ages 2–5)

REVIEWS: BL 10/15/99; 09/01/99; PW 05/17/99; CL

MacDonald, Suse. *A Was Once an Apple Pie.* Adapted and illustrated by the author. New York: Orchard Books, 2005.

From "A was once an apple pie" to "Z was once a little zebra," children will love this modern version of Edward Lear's nineteenth-century poem. With nonsense verses like "skunky, dunky, chunky skunky, stinky, stunky, little skunk," this read-aloud will bring smiles and laughter to all. (Ages 3–5)

REVIEWS: HBG 01/01/06; PW 08/15/05; SLJ 08/01/05; BL 08/01/05; CL

Martin, Bill, Jr. *Brown Bear, Brown Bear, What Do You See?* Illustrated by Eric Carle. New York: Henry Holt, 1983.

Brown bears, blue horses, purple cats, and black sheep see animals and beautiful children of various colors looking at them. This revision of a 1967 classic blends bold pictures, bright colors, and repetitive text to introduce colors, animals, and rhymes to a broad range of preschoolers. (Ages 2–5)

REVIEWS: HBG 03/01/97; HBG 09/01/92; SLJ 05/01/92; BL 03/01/92

Martin, Bill, Jr., and John Archambault. *Chicka Chicka Boom Boom.* Illustrated by Lois Ehlert. New York: Simon & Schuster, 1989.

> The adventure begins when all twenty-six letters of the alphabet race to the top of a coconut tree. Children of all ages will enjoy this colorful rhyming book filled with jazz-flavored phrases like "skit skat skoodle doot," accompanied by the unforgettable refrain, "Chicka chicka boom boom!" Librarians, teachers, and child-care providers should be prepared to read this delightful book again, and again, and again. (Ages 2–5)
>
> REVIEWS: SLJ 06/01/00; BL 03/15/90; BL 10/15/89; PW 10/13/89; BL 10/15/88; CL

Martin, Bill, Jr., and Michael Sampson. *Adam, Adam, What Do You See?* Illustrated by Cathie Felstead. Nashville, TN: Tommy Nelson, 2000.

> In the tradition of *Brown Bear, Brown Bear, What Do You See?* Adam, Noah, Joseph, Esther, Peter, and other well-known biblical figures are asked, "What do you see?" Each person replies, and the book, chapter, and verses where the story can be found in the Bible are conveniently referenced. Older preschoolers will be eager to hear each story in its entirety. (Ages 2–5)
>
> REVIEWS: SLJ, 12/01/00; PW 09/22/00

Martin, Bill, Jr., and Michael Sampson. *Chicka Chicka 1, 2, 3.* Illustrated by Lois Ehlert. New York: Simon & Schuster Books for Young Readers, 2004.

> As numbers one to ninety-nine race to the top of the apple tree, zero wonders, "Will there be a place for me?" Although the other numbers ignore zero as they romp and play, a swarm of bees make him a hero and prove that each number has a special place. As readers count from one to one hundred, they will enjoy the bold, colorful illustrations as well as the rhythm of the rhymes. (Ages 3–5)
>
> REVIEWS: HBG 04/01/05; HBM 09/01/04; SLJ 08/01/04; PW 07/19/04; BL 06/01/04; CL

Miranda, Anne. *To Market, to Market.* Illustrated by Janet Stevens. Orlando, FL: Red Wagon Books, 2007.

> Each time the brightly clad woman returns from the market, she has purchased an animal. When she returns with a goat, her frustration peaks when she realizes that the pig, lamb, cow, duck, hen, and goose

have taken over and destroyed her house. This new twist to a familiar rhyme will bring smiles to the faces of young readers. (Ages 4–5)

REVIEWS: HBG 10/01/07; PW 09/03/01; HBG 03/01/98; SLJ 01/01/98; BL 11/01/97; HBM 11/01/97; KR 10/15/97; PW 09/29/97; CL

Mitton, Tony. *Down by the Cool of the Pool.* Illustrated by Guy Parker-Rees. New York: Orchard Books, 2001.

While dancing down by the pool, Frog invites Duck, Pig, Sheep, Donkey, and many others to join him. Although they are not able to dance like Frog, they express their unique talents by flapping, wiggling, stamping, and drumming. The lively illustrations and energetic rhymes are sure to inspire readers and listeners of all ages to dance. (Ages 2–5)

REVIEWS: HBG 10/01/02; SLJ 07/01/02; KR 05/01/02; PW 04/15/02; CL

Nevius, Carol. *Building with Dad.* Illustrated by Bill Thomson. Tarrytown, NY: Marshall Cavendish, 2006.

When a father and son visit the construction site of a new school, the young boy experiences a world filled with bulldozers, rock spills, backhoes, trenches, graders, steamrollers, glops of cement, waxed floors, and more. Filled with vivid and realistic illustrations on elongated pages, readers will follow the project from the initial groundbreaking to the first day of school. (Ages 4–5)

REVIEWS: HBG 04/01/07; PW 10/09/06; SLJ 10/01/06; BL 09/01/06; CL

Newcome, Zita. *Head, Shoulders, Knees, and Toes: And Other Action Rhymes.* Illustrated by the author. Cambridge, MA: Candlewick Press, 2002.

Movement, singing, and fun are guaranteed as readers enjoy this collection of more than fifty songs, rhymes, and fingerplays. From the traditional "I'm a Little Teapot" and "Teddy Bear, Teddy Bear" to the modern "Boa Constrictor" and "One Man Went to Mow," children will delight in learning the accompanying body and finger motions. (Ages 2–5)

REVIEWS: HBG 04/01/03; SLJ 10/01/02; BL 09/15/02; PW 09/03/02; CL

Newman, Lesléa. *Where Is Bear?* Illustrated by Valeri Gorbachev. Orlando, FL: Gulliver Books, 2004.

Bunny covers her eyes and counts to ten as she and her forest friends engage in a game of hide-and-seek. When everyone except Bear is found, the animals begin to worry—where can Bear be? Turtle, Snake, Fox, and all the others work together to find their missing friend. (Ages 2–5)

REVIEWS: HBG 04/01/05; PW 11/01/04; SLJ 11/01/04; CL

Nunn, Daniel. *Counting 1 to 10.* Illustrated by Joanna Hinton-Malivoire. Chicago: Raintree, 2012.

Bright and bold illustrations and photographs of cupcakes, sunflowers, seashells, ducklings, striped socks, birthday candles, parrots, kites, and more entertain readers as they count from one to ten. In addition to a table of contents and index, this basic counting book includes a counting challenge young readers are sure to enjoy. (Ages 3–5)

REVIEWS: SLJ 04/01/12; CL

O'Keefe, Susan Heyboer. *Love Me, Love You.* Illustrated by Robin Spowart. Honesdale, PA: Boyds Mills Press, 2001.

Using soft pastel illustrations and flowing loving rhymes, a mother rabbit and her toddler demonstrate and express the unconditional love they have for each other. (Ages 2–4)

REVIEWS: HBG 10/01/01; BL 04/15/01; 04/01/01; CL

Oxenbury, Helen. *Clap Hands.* Illustrated by the author. New York: Simon & Schuster Children's Publishing Division, 1999.

Young children will delight as the spirited babies in this rhyming board book play, dance, eat, and more. Other Oxenbury books in this series include *All Fall Down, Say Goodnight,* and *Tickle, Tickle.* (Ages 0–3)

REVIEWS: CL

Peek-a-Boo What? Illustrated by Elliot Kreloff. New York: Begin Smart, 2009.

Simple rhymes; die-cut holes; foldout pages; and illustrations of dogs, fish, socks, and cows combine to make this an interactive treat for young readers. (Ages 1–2)

REVIEWS: BL 12/01/09

Rex, Michael. *Truck Duck.* Illustrated by the author. New York: G. P. Putnam's Sons, 2004.

In this rhyming book about transportation, ducks, crabs, cows, and chimps are driving trucks, cabs, plows, and blimps. (Ages 0–3)

REVIEWS: HBG 10/01/04; PW 02/02/04; SLJ 01/01/04; BL 01/01/04; CL

Rinker, Sherri Duskey. *Goodnight, Goodnight, Construction Site.* Illustrated by Tom Lichtenheld. San Francisco: Chronicle Books, 2011.

When the sun sets after a long, hard day at a construction site, even the equipment deserves a break. As the moon rises, this gentle story bids goodnight to the crane, cement mixer, dump truck, bulldozer, and excavator. *Goodnight, Goodnight, Construction Site* is the perfect bedtime story for lovers of big trucks. (Ages 1–5)

REVIEWS: HBG 10/01/11; BL 09/01/11; SLJ 07/01/11; PW 06/13/11

Root, Phyllis. *One Duck Stuck.* Illustrated by Jane Chapman. Cambridge, MA: Candlewick Press, 1998.

When a duck gets "stuck in the muck" down by the marsh, neighboring crickets, frogs, snails, snakes, and others respond to the call for help. As children listen to the sounds, rhythms, and rhymes of this whimsical tale, they will not be able to resist participating and chanting repeated phrases like "Help! Help! Who can help?" and "We can! We can!" (Ages 2–5)

REVIEWS: PW 01/20/03; HBG 09/01/98; SLJ 06/01/98; PW 05/04/98; CL

Schultz, Lucy. *Farm Faces: A Book of Masks.* Illustrated by Ann Martin Larranaga. Norwalk, CT: innovativeKids, 2006.

Using simple rhymes, this book introduces children to chicks, sheep, pigs, and other farm animals. When the book is open, strategically positioned holes create a mask, which makes the book an interactive delight for young preschoolers. Other notable titles in the iBaby series include *Zoo Faces: A Book of Masks* and *Goodnight Faces: A Book of Masks.* (Ages 0–3)

Seuss, Dr. *The Cat in the Hat.* Illustrated by the author. New York: Random House, 1985.

An unforgettable adventure begins when a cat, wearing a striped top hat and bowtie, visits two children and their fish on a cold and rainy day. (Ages 4–5)

REVIEWS: WLB 07/01/57; HB 06/01/57; SLJ 05/15/57; BL 05/01/57; CL

Seuss, Dr. *Green Eggs and Ham.* Illustrated by the author. New York: Beginner Books, 1988.

Sam-I-Am tirelessly pursues a fellow character and, after much determination, convinces him to try green eggs and ham. (Ages 3–5)

REVIEWS: WLB 01/01/61; BL 11/15/60; LJ 09/15/60

Seuss, Dr. *My Many Colored Days.* Illustrated by Steve Johnson and Lou Fancher. New York: Alfred A. Knopf, 1996.

From feel-good red days when a child kicks up his heels like a horse to purple days when he feels like a sad dinosaur that simply wants to groan and walk alone, rhyming text and dramatic abstract paintings combine colors and animals to introduce emotions to young readers. Written in a style not traditionally associated with Dr. Seuss, this is a book readers will love as they explore and discuss a variety of feelings, moods, and emotions. (Ages 2–5)

REVIEWS: HBG 03/01/97; SLJ 12/01/96; BL 11/01/96; KR 08/15/96; PW 07/22/96

Seuss, Dr. *One Fish, Two Fish, Red Fish, Blue Fish.* Illustrated by the author. New York: Beginner Books, 1988.

This collection of nonsense rhymes features memorable characters, including Mr. Gump and his seven-humped Wump, the Nook with a book on his hook, sleepwalking sheep, and a little girl who walks with cats on her head. (Ages 4–5)

REVIEWS: LJ 05/15/60; WLB 05/01/60

Shaw, Nancy. *Sheep in a Jeep.* Illustrated by Margot Apple. Boston: Houghton Mifflin, 1986.

The adventure begins when five sheep decide to take a ride in a red jeep on a sunny day. After encountering steep hills, gooey mud, and a messy accident, the sheep have no choice but to sell the jeep at a reduced cost. (Ages 2–5)

REVIEWS: PW 09/30/88; BL 05/01/87; PW 09/26/86; BL 09/01/86; PW 07/25/86

Shea, Susan A. *Do You Know Which Ones Will Grow?* Illustrated by Tom Slaughter. Maplewood, NJ: Blue Apple Books, 2011.

As preschoolers lift flaps and peep through die-cuts, they learn the difference between things that grow and things that remain the way they were initially made. This story in rhyme illustrates that although cubs, calves, piglets, and kits grow up to become bears, cows, pigs, and foxes, cars, stools, caps, and shovels do not grow and become trucks, chairs, hats, and plows. Children will enjoy answering yes or no to the questions presented to them. (Ages 4–5)

REVIEWS: HBG 10/01/11; SLJ 06/01/11; KR 04/01/11; PW 03/28/11; CL

Sierra, Judy. *Counting Crocodiles.* Illustrated by Will Hillenbrand. San Diego: Gulliver Books, 1997.

Based on an Asian trickster folktale, a sly monkey uses her ability to count to ten and back to one to trick a sea of crocodiles. As she counts, naive crocodiles form a bridge, allowing the monkey to journey from her lemon-tree island to an island flourishing with bananas. A fine blend of humor, movement, and rhyming verse crafts a book certain to be a read-aloud favorite. (Ages 3–5)

REVIEWS: PW 10/01/01; HBG 03/01/98; SLJ 10/01/97; BL 09/01/97; PW 06/30/97; CL

Silverman, Erica. *The Halloween House.* Illustrated by Jon Agee. New York: Farrar, Straus, & Giroux, 1997.

As two escaped prisoners take refuge in an old mansion on Halloween night, they encounter many spooky creatures occupying the house. Children will enjoy counting the rising vampires, swooping bats, dancing skeletons, and swinging spiders throughout the year. (Ages 3–5)

REVIEWS: PW 09/27/99; HBG 03/01/98; SLJ 11/01/97; HBM 09/01/07; BL 09/01/97; KR 07/01/97; CL

Slater, Dashka. *Baby Shoes.* Illustrated by Hiroe Nakata. New York: Bloomsbury Publishing, 2006.

As a young boy enjoys a day of romping around town with his mother, his brand-new white shoes become "speckled, spotted, polka-dotted, puddle-stomping, rainbow-romping" by the end of the day. Both readers and listeners will love the rhymes and rhythm of this book as green grass, purple plums, and brown mud adorn the boy's shoes. (Ages 2–5)

REVIEWS: HBG 10/01/06; SLJ 05/01/06; BL 05/01/06

Spicer, Maggee. *We'll All Go Sailing.* Illustrated by Richard Thompson. Allston, MA: Fitzhenry & Whiteside, 2001.

When the narrator and his friends Maggee and Jesse imagine sailing on seas of blue, black, red, green, and purple, they encounter uniquely colored sea creatures, such as purple sharks, green jellyfish, yellow seahorses, orange barracudas, and pink seals. The rhyming book concludes with its characters creating a book of the things they will see when they go sailing. After taking this colorful journey, readers may enjoy creating of book of their own. (Ages 3–5)

REVIEWS: SLJ 07/01/01; PW 06/04/01; BL 05/15/01; CL

Spurr, Elizabeth. *Farm Life.* Illustrated by Steve Björkman. New York: Holiday House, 2003.

As readers count barns of red, blue, green, brown, and gray and count balers, threshers, stallions, bales of hay, heifers, and piglets, they are introduced to the charms of traditional farm life. Since each scene begins with a question to the barn and ends with the phrase, "This is the farm life—but only a part," children will enjoy the repetition of the rhyming text. The book's glossary provides definitions for many farming terms that may be unfamiliar to many of today's youth. (Ages 3–5)

REVIEWS: HBG 10/01/03; SLJ 06/01/03; BL 03/15/03; PW 01/20/03; CL

Suen, Anastasia. *Subway.* Illustrated by Karen Katz. New York: Viking, 2004.

Simple rhyming text and cheery illustrations are used to chronicle a subway ride taken by a little girl and her mother. Repetition of words, like "walk, walk, walk" and "ride, ride, ride," combined with a diverse group of travelers, makes *Subway* a gratifying journey. (Ages 3–5)

REVIEWS: HBG 10/01/04; LJ 02/14/04; PW 02/02/04; SLJ 02/01/04; BL 02/01/04; CL

Taback, Simms. *This Is the House That Jack Built.* Illustrated by the author. New York: G. P. Putnam's Sons, 2002.

All of the familiar characters, plus a mystery guest, are present in Taback's modern version of this eighteenth-century cumulative story.

Mixed-media artwork fills each page with memorable color, energy, expression, and emotion. (Ages 4–5)

REVIEWS: PW 11/29/04; HBG 04/01/03; HBM 11/01/02; BL 10/01/02; SLJ 09/01/02; PW 07/22/02; KR 07/15/02; CL

Wadsworth, Olive A. *Over in the Meadow: A Counting Rhyme.* Illustrated by Anna Vojtech. New York: North-South Books, 2002.

The sounds and behaviors of meadow animals provide the backdrop for Vojtech's rendition of this familiar nineteenth-century rhyme. Children will enjoy counting from one to ten as turtles dig, rats gnaw, crows caw, and lizards bask. Older readers will delight in discovering ants, bugs, leaves, geese, and other countable animals and items nestled in the background. Ezra Jack Keats's *Over in the Meadow* (1999) is also a notable adaptation of the rhyme. (Ages 3–5)

REVIEWS: PW 08/25/03; HBG 10/01/02; 09/01/02; SLJ; 04/01/02; KR 02/01/02; CL

Walton, Rick. *So Many Bunnies: A Bedtime ABC and Counting Book.* Illustrated by Paige Miglio. New York: HarperFestival, 1998.

Classic Victorian-style illustrations by Paige Miglio add a twist to the familiar nursery rhyme "There Was an Old Woman Who Lived in a Shoe." As Old Mother Rabbit puts her twenty-six children to bed, she calls them each by name. From Abel who sleeps on a table to Zed who sleeps on the shed, children will enjoy the rhyme and repetition of the story, as well as the uniqueness of each child. (Ages 3–5)

REVIEWS: PW 12/24/01; HBG 09/01/98; BL 03/15/98; SLJ 03/01/98; KR 02/01/98; CL

Weeks, Sarah. *Mrs. McNosh Hangs Up Her Wash.* Illustrated by Nadine Bernard Westcott. St. Louis, MO: Turtleback Books, 2002.

A normal washing day becomes a hilarious tale as Mrs. McNosh washes and hangs out to dry unusual objects, including the dog, telephone, Grandpa's dentures, trash can, and turkey. After a long day, she lets her hair down and hangs herself up in a reclining chair. Preschoolers will enjoy the humorous illustrations and whimsical rhymes. (Ages 3–5)

REVIEWS: PW 04/01/02; HBG 09/01/98; SLJ 07/01/98; CL

Wheeler, Lisa. *Jazz Baby.* Illustrated by R. Gregory Christie. Orlando, FL: Harcourt, 2007.

Born into a family where older siblings tap and snap, Granny sings scat, Daddy sings low, Auntie toe taps, neighbors hip-hop, and bass players strum, how can the little one grow up to be anything but a jazz baby? Readers will enjoy sounds, rhythms, rhymes, and illustrations that finally put the jazz baby into a deep, deep sleep.

REVIEWS: SLJ 01/01/08; PW 11/19/07; BL 10/15/07; KR 10/15/07; CL

Williams, Sue. *I Went Walking.* Illustrated by Julie Vivas. New York: Gulliver Books, 1989.

A black cat, red cow, pink pig, and yellow dog are just a few of the animals a little boy meets as he begins a walk filled with color and mystery. The story concludes with an amusing two-page spread of the child frolicking with the six animals following him. As young listeners playfully repeat the rhythmic rhymes, colors and farm animals are identified. (Ages 3–5)

REVIEWS: PW 06/15/92; HBG 03/01/91; SLJ 10/01/90; BL 09/01/90; PW 08/31/90

Wilson, Karma. *A Frog in the Bog.* Illustrated by Joan Rankin. New York: Margaret K. McElderry Books, 2003.

While sitting on a log in the middle of the bog, a hungry frog grows larger and larger as he devours ticks, flies, snails, and other tasty treats. When the log turns out to be an alligator, the rhyming tale takes a humorous turn. (Ages 3–5)

REVIEWS: HBG 04/01/04; SLJ 12/01/03; BL 11/01/03; PW 10/20/03; CL

Wood, Audrey. *Silly Sally.* Illustrated by the author. San Diego: Harcourt, 1992.

Children will enjoy meeting the humorous characters Sally encounters as she travels to town "walking backwards, upside down." Preschoolers will want to hear this cumulative tale again and again. (Ages 3–5)

REVIEWS: HBG 09/01/92; SLJ 04/01/92; BL 03/15/92; KR 03/01/92; CL

Wood, Audrey. *Ten Little Fish.* Illustrated by Bruce Wood. New York: Blue Sky Press, 2004.

Ten brightly colored fish disappear one by one from the pages of this digitally created three-dimensional book as they dive, hide, grab a snack, and make a friend. Children with a complete understanding of the numbers one through ten will enjoy the *Finding Nemo*–like characters in this descending counting book. (Ages 4–5)

REVIEWS: HBG 04/01/05; SLJ 10/01/04; BL 08/01/04; PW 07/19/04

Zelinsky, Paul O. *Knick-Knack Paddywhack!* Illustrated by the author. New York: Dutton Children's Books, 2002

In this skillfully crafted toy and movable adaptation of the well-known folk song, readers of all ages will marvel at the animation experienced through pulling tabs, lifting and turning flaps, and spinning wheels. Children will count, laugh, clap, and sing for hours as these old men come rolling home. (Ages 2–5)

REVIEWS: HBG 04/01/03; HBM 01/01/03; SLJ 12/01/02; BL 11/01/02; KR 08/15/02; PW 08/12/02; CL

CHAPTER 4

Nursery Rhymes

Nursery Rhymes

Nursery rhymes transcend cultures and time because children love their language patterns and rhythm. As children hear and repeat the words, they discover the splendor of language. Many traditional rhymes like "Hey Diddle Diddle," "Baa Baa Black Sheep," "Little Bo Peep," and "Humpty Dumpty" are considered nursery rhymes and are credited to Mother Goose.

Crews, Nina. *The Neighborhood Mother Goose.* Photographed by the author. New York: Greenwillow Books, 2004.

> An urban setting and photographs of children and parents provide a modern setting for "Jack Be Nimble," "Georgie Porgie," "To Market, to Market," "Ride a Cockhorse," and other traditional favorites. (Ages 2–5)
>
> REVIEWS: HBG 10/01/04; HBM 05/01/04; PW 01/26/04; PW 01/09/04; SLJ 01/01/04; BL 12/01/03; CL

Duffy, Chris. *Nursery Rhyme Comics.* Illustrated by Patrick McDonnell et al. New York: First Second, 2011.

When fifty traditional and contemporary nursery rhymes like "Hush, Little Baby," "Mary Had a Little Lamb," "Jack and Jill," and "Solomon Grundy" are illustrated by fifty cartoonists and graphic artists—including Mo Oh, Sara Varon, Jaime Hernandez, and Mike Mignola—the result is this magnificent book with an innovative format that young children will enjoy and treasure. (Ages 3–5)

REVIEWS: HBG 04/01/12; BL 11/15/11; SLJ 09/01/11; KR 08/15/11; PW 08/01/11; CL

Hillenbrand, Will. *Mother Goose Picture Puzzles.* Illustrated by the author. Tarrytown, NY: Marshall Cavendish Children, 2011.

Using rebuses and vibrant illustrations, preschoolers are challenged to interactively recite "The Pumpkin-Eater," "Little Boy Blue," "Wee Willie Winkie," "There Was an Old Lady," and sixteen additional traditional nursery rhymes. (Ages 4–5).

REVIEWS: HBG 10/01/11; SLJ 04/01/11; BL 03/01/11; KR 02/01/11; CL

Hines, Anna Grossnickle. *1, 2, Buckle My Shoe.* Illustrated by the author. Orlando, FL: Harcourt, 2008.

Quilt patches detailed with buttons and bold numbers make this version of a favorite nursery rhyme memorable to preschoolers. (Ages 1–3)

REVIEWS: BL 05/15/08; SLJ 05/01/08; KR 04/15/08; CL

Itsy Bitsy Spider. Illustrated by Annie Kubler. Auburn, ME: Child's Play, 2004.

While singing this beloved nursery rhyme, young children will also learn simple sign language. *Itsy Bitsy Spider* is simply one familiar rhyme in the Sign and Singalong series. Others include *Twinkle, Twinkle, Little Star*, *Teddy Bear, Teddy Bear*, and *Baa, Baa, Black Sheep*. (Ages 0–3)

REVIEWS: SLJ 10/01/05; PW 05/30/05; CL

Jay, Alison. *Red Green Blue: A First Book of Colors.* Illustrated by the author. New York: Dutton Children's Books, 2010.

As children learn colors and are briefly introduced to characters from familiar nursery rhymes, they will enjoy encountering Miss Muffet's black spider, Old Mother Hubbard's orange cupboard, and the golden palace of Old King Cole. With the turn of each page, characters from the twenty rhymes come to life and interact with one another thanks to Jay's radiant crackle-varnish illustrations. After reading this delightful book, youngsters will surely want to hear and learn each rhyme in its entirety. (Ages 2–5)

REVIEWS: HBG 10/01/10; SLJ 06/01/10; PW 04/26/10; CL

Long, Sylvia. *Sylvia Long's Mother Goose.* Illustrated by the author. San Francisco: Chronicle Books, 1999.

In this collection of more than eighty traditional and lesser-known nursery rhymes, Long uses pen-and-ink and watercolor illustrations to suggest unique interpretations of some of world's most beloved rhymes. (Ages 1–5)

REVIEWS: HBG 04/01/00; LJ 12/01/99; SLJ 12/01/99; PW 10/04/99; CL

Marshall, James. *James Marshall's Mother Goose.* Illustrated by the author. New York: Farrar, Straus, & Giroux, 1979.

Marshall's humorous characters bring "Here We Go Round the Mulberry Bush," "Little Boy Blue," "Jack Sprat," "Old Mother Hubbard," and many additional familiar nursery rhymes alive. (Ages 3–5)

REVIEWS: PW 11/28/86

Moses, Will. *Mother Goose.* Illustrated by the author. New York: Philomel Books, 2003.

After six nursery rhymes are introduced, double-page oil paintings combine the previous rhymes to create a memorable folk-art illustration. As the books cover indicates, these sixty Mother Goose rhymes, accompanied by twelve paintings, create "a joyful collection of classic nursery rhymes and riddles to delight little people." (Ages 2–5)

REVIEWS: HBG 04/01/04; SLJ 09/01/03; BL 08/01/03; PW 07/21/03; CL

Mother Goose: Numbers on the Loose. Compiled and illustrated by Leo Dillon and Diane Dillon. Orlando, FL: Harcourt, 2007.

In this collection of more than twenty Mother Goose number rhymes, vibrant, detailed illustrations introduce preschoolers to both familiar and lesser-known nursery rhymes, including "Baa, Baa, Black Sheep,"

"One, Two, Buckle My Shoe," "From Wibbleton to Wobbleton," and "Gregory Griggs." (Ages 3–5)

REVIEWS: HBM 11/01/07; PW 10/08/07; SLJ 10/01/07; BL 09/01/07; CL

My First Nursery Rhymes. Illustrated by Bruce Whatley. New York: HarperFestival, 1999.

Simple, humorous illustrations introduce "Hey Diddle Diddle," "Hickory Dickory Dock," "Humpty Dumpty," and seven additional beloved nursery rhymes to young children. (Ages 1–4)

REVIEWS: HBG 09/01/99; SLJ 04/01/99; BL 02/01/99; KR 12/15/98; CL

Newcome, Zita. *Toddlerobics: Fun Action Rhymes.* Illustrated by the author. Cambridge, MA: Candlewick Press, 2002.

Nursery rhymes like "Row, Row, Row Your Boat," "Pat-a-Cake," "This Is the Way the Lady Rides," and "If You're Happy and You Know It" come alive as readers pull tabs and turn wheels in this fun-filled pop-up book. (Ages 3–5)

REVIEWS: PW 10/28/02; CL

Opie, Iona. *Here Comes Mother Goose.* Illustrated by Rosemary Wells. Cambridge, MA: Candlewick Press, 1999.

A family of playful guinea pigs leads readers through a collection of Mother Goose favorites. The oversize pages and bold, familiar artwork of Wells make this a lap book children will cherish for many years. (Ages 2–5)

REVIEWS: HBG 04/01/00; HBM 12/01/99; KR 11/01/99; PW 10/04/99; SLJ 10/01/99; CL

Opie, Iona. *Mother Goose's Little Treasures.* Illustrated by Rosemary Wells. Cambridge, MA: Candlewick Press, 2007.

"Handy Spandy," "Parcel Post," "Little Fatty Doctor," and "Little Old Dog Sits under a Chair" are just a few of the less familiar nursery rhymes introduced in this collection. Combined with watercolor and gouache pictures by renowned illustrator Rosemary Wells, the rhymes will be eagerly received by preschool children. (Ages 3–5)

REVIEWS: BL 09/01/07; SLJ 09/01/07; PW 08/20/07

Ross, Tony. *Three Little Kittens and Other Favorite Nursery Rhymes.* Selected and illustrated by the author. New York: Henry Holt, 2009.

Humorous illustrations adorn each page of this oversize book as children are introduced to almost fifty traditional and modern nursery rhymes. (Ages 3–6)

REVIEWS: SLJ 04/01/09; PW 03/16/09; KR 03/01/09; BL 02/01/09

Spirin, Gennady. *A Apple Pie.* Illustrated by the author. New York: Philomel Books, 2005.

Based on a seventeenth-century English nursery rhyme, Spirin's watercolor illustrations uses both upper- and lowercase letters to follow the adventure of an apple pie from A to Z. Children of various ages will enjoy this eloquent adaptation. (Ages 2–5)

REVIEWS: HBG 04/01/06; BL 11/01/05; SLJ 09/01/05; KR 08/15/05; PW 08/15/05; CL

Yaccarino, Dan. *Mother Goose.* Illustrated by the author. New York: Random House, 2004.

Using the city as its backdrop, Yaccarino's humorous illustrations put a fresh spin on both traditional and nontraditional nursery rhymes. Adults will also chuckle while reading each rhyme. (Ages 2–5)

REVIEWS: HBG 04/01/05; BL 10/15/04; SLJ 10/01/04; PW 09/06/04; CL

Ziefert, Harriet. *Where Is Humpty Dumpty?* Illustrated by Laura Rader. New York: Sterling Publishing, 2004.

As readers turn the sturdy, split pages of this flip-and-read book, rhymes and illustrations reveal five Mother Goose favorites, including "Hey Diddle Diddle" and "Humpty Dumpty." Another notable flip-and-read book is *What Happened to Jack and Jill?* (Ages 3–5)

CHAPTER 5

Fingerplays and Action Rhymes

Key to Review Sources

BL *Booklist*; **CL** *Children's Literature* (reviews searchable in *Children's Literature Comprehensive Database*); **HBG** *Horn Book Guide*; **HBM** *Horn Book Magazine*; **KR** *Kirkus Reviews*; **LJ** *Library Journal*; **PW** *Publisher's Weekly*; **SLJ** *School Library Journal*; **WLB** *Wilson Library Bulletin*

Some book reviews predate the edition of books because reviews refer to earlier editions.

Fingerplays and Action Rhymes

Fingerplays and action rhymes are songs, rhymes, games, or poems dramatized by hand, finger, or body motions as they are recited or sung. Many of these books include instructions and musical arrangements along with the words. In addition to developing listening, fine-motor, memory, and recall skills, fingerplays and action rhymes teach preschoolers spatial concepts (such as up, down, front, back, in, and out) and to follow directions.

Brown, Marc. *Hand Rhymes.* Illustrated by the author. New York: Dutton Children's Books, 1985.

> In an iconic style, Brown illustrates a collection of fourteen traditional and modern hand rhymes. Readers will find the detailed hand and body diagrams useful as they teach energetic gestures to youngsters. (Ages 3–5)
>
> *REVIEWS:* PW 11/25/85; SLJ 11/01/85

Griego, Margot C., Betsy L. Bucks, Sharon S. Gilbert, and Laurel H. Kimball. *Tortillitas para mamá and Other Nursery Rhymes.* Illustrated by Barbara Cooney. New York: Henry Holt, 1981.

Collected from Spanish communities, this collection of traditional nursery rhymes, action rhymes, and lullabies is presented in both Spanish and English.

REVIEWS: PW 03/13/87

Hayes, Sarah. *Clap Your Hands: Finger Rhymes.* Illustrated by Toni Goffe. New York: Lothrop, Lee, & Shepard Books, 1988.

Preschoolers will eagerly follow the finger movements in this collection of twenty-three traditional and modern fingerplays, including "Here Is the Church," "Three Little Monkeys," "Ten Fat Sausages," and "Pat-a-Cake." (Ages 2–5)

REVIEWS: BL 03/15/88; PW 03/11/88

If You're Happy and You Know It. Illustrated by Brenda Sexton. New York: Cartwheel Books, 2006. (Ages 0–3)

Based on the familiar children's song, this sturdy book in the My First Taggies series has a quilted front cover and looped ribbon tags attached to each page. As youngsters sing this familiar action rhyme, they will enjoy rubbing the cover and chewing, pulling, and turning pages with the tags. (Ages 0–3)

REVIEWS: CL

Kovalski, Maryann. *The Wheels on the Bus.* Illustrated by the author. Boston: Little, Brown, 1987.

As Grandma, Jenny, and Joanna wait at the bus stop, they sing the familiar fingerplay to pass the time. Older preschoolers familiar with the fingerplay will especially enjoy this adaptation. (Ages 4–5)

REVIEWS: PW 09/28/90; BL 12/15/87; SLJ 11/01/87; PW 10/30/87

Kubler, Annie. *Itsy Bitsy Spider.* Illustrated by the author. Auburn, ME: Child's Play, 2004.

While singing this beloved nursery rhyme, young children will also learn simple sign language. Itsy Bitsy Spider is simply one familiar rhyme in the Sign and Singalong series. Others include *Twinkle, Twinkle, Little Star, Teddy Bear, Teddy Bear*, and *Baa, Baa, Black Sheep.* (Ages 0–3)

REVIEWS: SLJ 10/01/05; PW 05/30/05; CL

Newcome, Zita. *Head, Shoulders, Knees, and Toes: And Other Action Rhymes.* Illustrated by the author. Cambridge, MA: Candlewick Press, 2002.

Movement, singing, and fun are guaranteed as readers enjoy this collection of more than fifty songs, rhymes, and fingerplays. From the traditional "I'm a Little Teapot" and "Teddy Bear, Teddy Bear" to the modern "Boa Constrictor" and "One Man Went to Mow," children will delight in learning the accompanying body and finger motions. (Ages 2–5)

REVIEWS: HBG 04/01/03; SLJ 10/01/02; BL 09/15/02; PW 09/03/02; CL

Oxenbury, Helen. *Clap Hands.* Illustrated by the author. New York: Simon & Schuster Children's Publishing, 1999.

Young children will delight as the spirited babies in this rhyming board book, play, dance, eat, and more. Other Oxenbury books in this series include *All Fall Down, Say Goodnight*, and *Tickle, Tickle.* (Ages 0–3)

REVIEWS: CL

Yolen, Jane. *This Little Piggy: Lap Songs, Finger Plays, Clapping Games, and Pantomime Rhymes.* Illustrated by Will Hillenbrand. Musical Arrangements by Adam Stemple. Cambridge, MA: Candlewick Press, 2005.

This oversize collection of songs, fingerplays, games, and rhymes includes "There Was an Old Woman," "Coventry Cross," "Where Is Thumbkin?" "Pease Porridge Hot," "I'm a Little Teapot," and more traditional favorites. Charming mixed-media illustrations and the accompanying sing-along CD are sure to make youngsters clap, giggle, wiggle, and sing, time and time again. (Ages 1–4)

REVIEWS: PW 05/29/06; SLJ 02/01/06; BL 01/01/06; CL

CHAPTER 6

Board Books

Board Books

The thick pages of board books provide handling ease to young hands as children hold these books and turn the pages. Although most board books are made of cardboard or cloth over board with stiff, sturdy covers, many are soft and even washable. Many titles annotated in other chapters of this book are also available in board editions.

Alborough, Jez. *Hug.* Cambridge, MA: Candlewick Press, 2000.

Walking through the jungle alone, a sad chimpanzee comes to tears as he sees elephants, snakes, lions, and other animals embracing lovingly. His sadness is replaced by joy, however, when his mother arrives and gives the chimp the tender hug he both desires and deserves. Rounds of hugs are in store for all the animals as this tender story concludes. (Ages 2–5)

REVIEWS: PW 10/17/05; HBG 10/01/02; PW 12/03/01; HBG 04/01/01; SLJ 12/01/00; PW 11/20/00; KR 11/01/00; CL

Baker, Keith. *Little Green.* Illustrated by the author. New York: Red Wagon Books, 2005.

A young boy paints the flight of a green hummingbird zipping, jigging, jagging, dipping, sipping, dashing, darting, zigging, and zagging outside his window. Baker combines a calming garden view and simple, lively rhyming text to create a gratifying story. (Ages 2–5)

REVIEWS: PW 02/28/05; HBG 10/01/01; BL 04/15/01; SLJ 04/01/01; KR 03/01/01; PW 02/12/01; CL

Bang, Molly. *Ten, Nine, Eight.* Illustrated by the author. New York: Tupelo Books, 1996.

The reader counts from ten to one as a father prepares his daughter for bed. The award-winning illustrations depict the warmth of a child's room (soft toys, snow falling through open windowpanes, and a mobile made of beautiful shells) and the wonder of love shared between a father and daughter. This book is sure to be a bedtime favorite. (Ages 2–4)

REVIEWS: BL 11/15/98; PW 05/03/91; BL 12/15/89; CL

Barton, Byron. *My Car.* Illustrated by the author. New York: HarperFestival, 2003.

Sam loves his bright red car and is eager to share his affection for it with preschoolers. Readers will learn many facts about cars, from keeping them clean to driving them to work. Automobile enthusiasts will be overjoyed to discover that Sam drives a bus for a living. (Ages 2–5)

REVIEWS: PW 07/19/04; HBG 04/01/02; HBM 11/01/01; HBG 11/01/01; SLJ 08/01/01; PW 07/01/01; BL 07/01/01; KR 06/15/01; CL

Bathtime Peekaboo! New York: DK Publishing, 2005.

Readers are encouraged to lift the flaps and feel scaly fish, bumpy starfish, smooth ducks, cuddly penguins, and squishy frogs as bath time approaches. (Ages 1–5)

REVIEWS: PW 08/08/05

Carle, Eric. *Do You Want to Be My Friend?* New York: HarperCollins, 1995.

A lonely gray mouse searches for a friend. As he eagerly chases the tails of horses, lions, monkeys, peacocks, and other contenders, he is unaware that his biggest predator is present throughout the book. *Do You Want to Be My Friend?* is a timeless book by one of children's literature's most beloved illustrators. (Ages 2–5)

REVIEWS: PW 08/14/95; CL

Carle, Eric. *My Very First Book of Colors.* Illustrated by the author. New York: Philomel Books, 2005.

In this toy and movable book, children are challenged to match pictures on the bottom half of the page with colors on the top half of the page. Levels of difficulty range from simple (brown shoes) to somewhat complex (a multicolored butterfly). (Ages 2–5)

REVIEWS: CL

Carle, Eric. *My Very First Book of Shapes.* Illustrated by the author. New York: Philomel Books, 2005.

In this toy and movable book, children are challenged to match pictures on the bottom half of the page with corresponding shapes on the top half of the page. Levels of difficulty range from simple circles and squares to somewhat complex shapes such as squiggles and crescents. (Ages 2–5)

REVIEWS: PW 04/25/05; CL

Carle, Eric. *The Very Lonely Firefly.* Illustrated by the author. New York: Philomel Books, 1995.

A lonely firefly encounters lightbulbs, candles, lanterns, fireworks, and other luminous things before meeting a group of fireflies. Carle's cut-paper collages and battery-powered flashing fireflies make this book a joy. (Ages 1–5)

REVIEWS: HBG 04/01/00; HBG 09/01/95; SLJ 08/01/95; PW 06/05/95; KR 06/01/95; BL 05/15/95; CL

Carle, Eric. *The Very Quiet Cricket.* Illustrated by the author. New York: Philomel Books, 1990.

When a young cricket encounters locusts, spittlebugs, cicadas, bumblebees, and mosquitoes, who all greet him with their unique sounds, he tries to return their greeting by rubbing his wings together and chirping. Unfortunately, nothing happens. As he matures and meets a female cricket, he tries again. This time he makes the most beautiful sound the female cricket has ever heard. Readers will enjoy the battery-powered chirping sound the last page makes. (Ages 1–5)

REVIEWS: HBG 09/01/97; HBG 03/01/91; SLJ 12/01/90; PW 11/19/90; PW 11/9/90; BL 10/01/90; CL

Christian, Cheryl. *Where Does It Go?/¿Dónde va?* Photographed by Laura Dwight. New York: Star Bright Books, 2004.

As readers turn pages and lift flaps, they will learn where diapers, shoes, hats, bears, and books belong. Additional titles in this bilingual series include *Where's the Puppy?/¿Dónde está el perrito? How Many?/¿Cuántos hay?* and *What Happens Next?/Y ahora, ¿qué pasará?* (Ages 0–3)

REVIEWS: CL

Crews, Donald. *Inside Freight Train.* Illustrated by the author. New York: HarperFestival, 2001.

As readers explore engines, cattle cars, refrigerator cars, stock cars, and more, cardboard doors slide open, revealing the items, animals, and people commonly found on freight trains. (Ages 1–3)

REVIEWS: HBG 10/01/01; PW 02/19/01; BL 12/15/00; CL

Cummings, Pat. *My Aunt Came Back.* Illustrated by the author. New York: HarperFestival, 1998.

Each time a young girl's aunt returns from an exotic location, she brings her niece memorable gifts like wooden shoes, quilted vests, painted fans, parasols, rings of gold, and berets. Before visiting Kathmandu, the aunt gives her niece a gift she will always cherish—a chance to travel to Kathmandu with her. Toddlers will enjoy repeating the rhyming words and sounds. (Ages 2–5)

REVIEWS: SLJ 10/01/98; HBG 09/01/98; CL

Curious George: Before and After. Boston: Houghton Mifflin, 2006.

As readers turn pages and lift flaps, they will take an adventure with George as he experiences how it feels to be hungry and full, go up and down, and be dirty and clean. About more than simply opposites, this colorful and sophisticated book in rhyme also teaches sequence and consequences. (Ages 1–3)

REVIEWS: CL

Dunrea, Olivier. *Gossie.* Illustrated by the author. New York: Houghton Mifflin Company, 2002.

Gossie is a gosling who loves to wear bright red boots every day wherever she goes. When Gossie wakes up one morning and cannot find her beloved boots, she is heartbroken to say the least. Then she meets Gertie, another gosling who loves boots—Gertie had borrowed Gossie's boots. It is easy to see how these boot-loving goslings became friends for life. *Gossie and Gertie* is another notable book featuring these lovable characters. (Ages 2–5)

REVIEWS: PW 01/22/07; HBG 04/01/03; HBM 01/01/03; SLJ 09/01/02; BL 08/01/02; PW 07/15/02; KR 06/15/02; CL

Dunrea, Olivier. *Ollie.* Illustrated by the author. New York: Houghton Mifflin, 2003.

The gosling Ollie refuses to hatch. No matter how much Gossie and Gertie try to persuade him, he rolls, hides, and screams from his egg, "I won't come out!" When the older goslings give up and say, "Don't come out," Ollie finally decides to emerge from his egg. Preschoolers of all ages will relate to Ollie's defiant attitude. *Ollie the Stomper* is another notable title starring this unabashed gosling. (Ages 1–4)

REVIEWS: PW 04/16/07; SLJ 10/01/04; HBG 04/01/04; BL 10/01/03; PW 07/14/03; SLJ 07/01/03; CL

Ehlert, Lois. *Eating the Alphabet.* Illustrated by the author. San Diego: Harcourt, 1996.

Lois Ehlert takes readers on a colorful discovery of the alphabet through both common and exotic fruits and vegetables, such as onions, peas, and bananas, as well as *xiguas*, jicamas, and kohlrabies. In addition to learning the alphabet, youngsters will be encouraged by the bold and enticing illustrations to acquaint themselves with both well-known and unfamiliar fruits and vegetables. (Ages 0–3)

REVIEWS: HBG 09/01/96; BL 04/01/96; HB 05/01/89; SLJ 05/01/89; BL 03/15/89; PW 03/10/89; CL

Ehlert, Lois. *Fish Eyes: A Book You Can Count On.* Illustrated by the author. New York: Red Wagon Books, 1990.

> After imagining being a fish, children are taken on an underwater journey, where they see and count a variety of brightly colored fish. Ehlert's rhyming counting book will amuse early counters. (Ages 3–5)
>
> REVIEWS: PW 06/15/92; HBG 09/01/90; SLJ 05/01/90; PW 04/13/90; BL 03/01/90; CL

Ehlert, Lois. *Hands.* Illustrated by the author. New York: Harcourt Brace, 1997.

> In this glove-shaped book, Ehlert describes how she and her parents used their hands and tools during her childhood. As her father built things in his workshop and her mother made crafts and clothes, the author would enjoy crafting and painting. Gardening was something they all enjoyed doing. Readers will enjoy the superior design of this book, including the flaps, foldout pages, and gloves. (Ages 4–5)
>
> REVIEWS: HBG 03/01/98; SLJ 12/01/97; BL 11/15/97; KR 07/15/97; PW 06/30/97

Emma Treehouse Ltd. *My Pets.* Illustrated by Caroline Davis. Wilton, CT: Tiger Tales, 2007.

> With the aid of chunky, sturdy tabs, young preschoolers lift flaps to lend a hand as a girl searches for her pet rabbit, cat, and dog. Other notable titles in the Easy Flaps series include *My Babies*, *My Friends*, and *My Toys*. (Ages 0–2)
>
> REVIEWS: CL

Falconer, Ian. *Olivia Counts.* Illustrated by the author. New York: Atheneum Books for Young Readers, 2002.

> Toddlers will enjoy counting from one to ten with Olivia, a charming piglet. In bold three-color illustrations, children will join Olivia as she counts balls, aunts, books, toys, and more. The book concludes with ten Olivias engaging in activities like jumping rope, hammering a nail, wearing panty hose, and performing a handstand. (Ages 0–3)
>
> REVIEWS: HBG 10/01/02; BL 07/01/02; SLJ 06/01/02; PW 05/06/02; KR 05/01/02; CL

Fleming, Denise. *The Everything Book.* Illustrated by the author. New York: Henry Holt, 2000.

> This collection of rhymes, colors, shapes, letters, numbers, seasons, and more offers readers something new each time they read the book. (Ages 2–5)
>
> REVIEWS: PW 08/02/04; HBG 04/01/01; SLJ 10/01/00; PW 08/04/00; BL 07/27/00; BL 07/01/00; KR 06/15/00: CL

Ford, Bernette. *No More Diapers for Ducky!* Illustrated by Sam Williams. New York: Boxer Books, 2007.

> When Ducky realizes that Piggy uses the potty instead of wearing a diaper like the cold and wet one she is currently wearing, she decides it is time to try the potty as well. This nonthreatening toilet-training tale is ideal for children who are ready to make this momentous transition. (Ages 2–4)
>
> REVIEWS: SLJ 08/01/06; BL 06/01/06; PW 03/27/06; CL

Frazee, Marla. *Hush, Little Baby: A Folk Song with Pictures.* Illustrated by the author. Orlando, FL: Red Wagon Books, 2007.

> In this story based on the well-known lullaby, an older sibling encourages her parents and others to soothe the wailing baby with a mockingbird, diamond ring, billy goat, and horse and cart. Amazingly, the baby stops bawling when the horse and cart tumble down a hill, and the baby returns to being "the sweetest little baby in town." Filled with expressive illustrations, *Horn Book Magazine* calls this "the sweetest—and definitely savviest—little version of this particular lullaby to date." (Ages 0–3)
>
> REVIEWS: PW 04/16/07; PW 09/08/03; HBG 04/01/00; HBM 12/01/99; LJ 12/01/99; BL 11/15/99; SLJ 10/01/99; PW 08/30/99; KR 08/15/99; CL

Fry, Sonali. *My Busy Day.* Photographed by Ken Karp Photography. New York: Simon & Schuster Children's Publishing, 2006.

> As the children in the book get dressed, eat, play with toys, visit the park, and prepare for bed, readers can interact with them by tying ribbons on dresses, touching shiny boots, seeing their reflections in silverware, and rubbing soft towels. The sturdy handle makes this a book tod-

dlers will enjoy carrying from place to place. *My Busy Day* is one of the notable titles in Baby Nick Jr.'s Curious Buddies series. (Ages 1–3)

REVIEWS: CL

Guettier, Bénédicte. *In the Jungle . . .* Illustrated by the author. La Jolla, CA: Kane/Miller Book Publishers, 2002.

By placing their faces in large cutout circles, readers instantly transform into bears, elephants, crocodiles, monkeys, and other familiar zoo animals. (Ages 0–3)

REVIEWS: PW 10/21/02; CL

Heck, Ed. *Big Fish Little Fish.* Illustrated by the author. New York: Price Stern Sloan, 2007.

With the use of simple text and bold, bright illustrations, youngsters explore several spatial concepts, such as big, little, front, above, inside, and fast, as an entertaining underwater adventure unfolds. (Ages 2–5)

REVIEWS: PW 08/20/07

Hest, Amy. *Kiss Good Night.* Illustrated by Anita Jeram. Cambridge, MA: Candlewick Press, 2004

It's bedtime for Sam, and his mother has read his favorite story, tucked him in, arranged his stuffed animals, and joined him in a glass of warm milk—what else does he want before going to sleep? A few goodnight kisses, of course. (Ages 2–5)

REVIEWS: PW 11/08/04; HBG 04/01/02; SLJ 11/01/01; BL 10/01/01; KR 08/15/01; PW 08/06/01

Hoban, Tana. *1, 2, 3.* Photographed by the author. New York: Greenwillow Books, 1985.

Bold photographs of familiar objects such as shoes, blocks, fingers, and animal crackers are used to introduce the very young to numbers and the concept of counting. (Ages 0–2)

Hoban, Tana. *Red, Blue, Yellow Shoe.* Photographed by the author. New York: Greenwillow Books, 1986.

Bold photographs of familiar objects and animals, such as shoes, leaves, teddy bears, and cats, introduce colors to the very young. (Ages 0–2)

REVIEWS: SLJ 12/01/96; PW 11/28/86; BL 10/01/86

Hubbell, Patricia. *Wrapping Paper Romp.* Illustrated by Jennifer Plecas. New York: HarperFestival, 1998.

As a toddler unwraps a present, readers quickly realize that a creative mind and brightly colored wrapping paper and tissue paper can be just as much fun as the actual gift. Children age one and older will find the smooth rhyming couplets and joyous illustrations between the covers of this book delightful. (Ages 1–5)

REVIEWS: SLJ 02/01/99; CL

If You're Happy and You Know It. Illustrated by Brenda Sexton. New York: Cartwheel Books, 2006.

Based on the familiar children's song, this sturdy book in the My First Taggies series has a quilted front cover and looped ribbon tags attached to each page. As youngsters sing this familiar action rhyme, they will enjoy rubbing the cover and chewing, pulling, and turning pages with the tags. (Ages 0–3)

REVIEWS: CL

James, Simon. *Little One Step.* Illustrated by the author. Cambridge, MA: Candlewick Press, 2003.

When the youngest of three lost ducklings feels he cannot go any further, his older brother introduces him to a technique called one step. By concentrating on taking one step at a time, the little duckling, affectionately nicknamed "Little One Step," is the first of the brothers to reach their mother. *Little One Step* is an excellent introduction to the power of perseverance. (Ages 1–4)

REVIEWS: SLJ 10/01/04; HBG 10/01/03; SLJ 04/01/03; BL 03/15/03; PW 03/03/03; KR 02/01/03; CL

Jay, Alison. *1, 2, 3: A Child's First Counting Book.* Illustrated by the author. New York: Dutton Children's Books, 2009.

As children count to ten and back again, they encounter characters from more than fifteen of their favorite fairy tales, including "Cinderella," "The Princess and the Pea," "Hansel and Gretel," "The Gingerbread Man," and "Jack and the Beanstalk." Jay's magnificent crackle-glaze paintings breathe life into each word and fairy tale. (Ages 1–5)

REVIEWS: BL 09/15/07; PW 09/03/07; SLJ 09/01/07

Laden, Nina. *Peek-a-Who?* Illustrated by the author. San Francisco: Chronicle Books, 2000.

> Simple rhyming text and die-cut windows make this the ideal guessing book for preschool children. The mirrored end page, appropriately captioned, "Peek a YOU!" is sure to delight young readers again and again. (Ages 0–2)
>
> REVIEWS: SLJ 07/01/00

Lewis, Kevin. *Chugga-Chugga Choo-Choo.* Illustrated by Daniel Kirk. New York: Hyperion Books for Children, 1999.

> From sunup until bedtime, children will enjoy riding this steam engine as it journeys through the country, around mountains, into tunnels, and across rivers to deliver a freight of toys to the city. Preschoolers are sure to make train sounds while reading the book. (Ages 2–5)
>
> REVIEWS: BL 10/15/99; 09/01/99; PW 05/17/99; CL

Marzollo, Jean. *I Spy Little Numbers.* Illustrated by Walter Wick. New York: Scholastic, 1999.

> In this book, young children will learn numbers, colors, and shapes as they search for objects hidden within the brightly colored photographs. Delightful rhyming text combined with simple and bold illustrations make this a book children will return to again and again. (Ages 2–5)
>
> REVIEWS: CL

Miranda, Anne. *To Market, to Market.* Illustrated by Janet Stevens. Orlando: Red Wagon Books, 2007.

> Each time the brightly clad woman returns from the market, she has purchased an animal. When she returns with a goat, her frustration peaks when she realizes that the pig, lamb, cow, duck, hen, and goose have taken over and destroyed her house. This new twist to a familiar rhyme will bring smiles to the faces of young readers. (Ages 4–5)
>
> REVIEWS: HBG 10/01/07; PW 09/03/01; HBG 03/01/98; SLJ 01/01/98; BL 11/01/97; HBM 11/01/97; KR 10/15/97; PW 09/29/97; CL

Murphy, Mary. *I Kissed the Baby!* Illustrated by the author. Cambridge, MA: Candlewick Press, 2003.

Excite builds as a baby duck is sung to, tickled, and kissed by various animals, including her mother. And Mother Duck kisses her duckling over and over again. This is a memorable story for young preschoolers. (Ages 0–3)

REVIEWS: PW 12/06/04; HBG 10/01/03; HBM 07/01/03; SLJ 05/01/03; PW 04/07/03; BL 04/01/03; CL

Parr, Todd. *The Best Friends Book.* Illustrated by the author. New York: Megan Tingley Books, 2005.

No one but a best friend will say, "You look good even if you have a bad haircut," or let you play with a doll "even if you pull her arm off." Filled with humor, this book teaches the true meaning of the word *friendship.* (Ages 4–5)

REVIEWS: HBG 09/01/00; SLJ 08/01/00; KR 01/15/00

Peek-a-Boo What? Illustrated by Elliot Kreloff. New York: Begin Smart, 2009.

Simple rhymes; die-cut holes; foldout pages; and illustrations of dogs, fish, socks, and cows combine to make this an interactive treat for young readers. (Ages 1–2)

REVIEWS: BL 12/01/09

Petty, Colin. *Colors.* Illustrated by the author. Hauppauge, NY: Barron's Educational Series, 2005.

As children place a finger in a small hole and slide it to the left or right, the answer to the question, "What color?" appears in a cutout box on the corresponding page. As one of the four titles in the Concept Sliders series, *Colors* is an entertaining way to introduce basic colors to youngsters. (Ages 1–3)

REVIEWS: PW 08/28/06

Saltzberg, Barney. *Beautiful Oops!* Illustrated by the author. New York: Workman Publishing, 2010.

While examining torn pages, spills, bent pages, smudges and smears, holes, and more, readers will see the beauty and creative opportunities that mistakes and imperfections offer. Preschoolers will enjoy the bright, bold illustrations as they lift flaps and as holes spiral toward them. (Ages 3–5)

REVIEWS: KR 12/01/10; PW 08/23/10; CL

Sawyer, Parker K. *Potty Time!* Illustrated by Christopher Moroney. New York: Random House, 2006.

Join Grover and many of his Sesame Street friends as they explore and share their experiences with a large white porcelain fixture in the bathroom—the toilet. On the final page of the book, children can share in Grover's excitement of using the potty for the first time by moving the tab on the toilet to simulate flushing. (Ages 2–3)

REVIEWS: CL

Schachner, Judy. *Skippyjon Jones Shape Up.* Illustrated by the author. New York: Dutton Children's Books, 2008.

Skippyjon Jones, America's favorite Siamese kitty boy, stays in shape with shapes as he runs in circles, salsa dances on squares, reaches for stars, rocks back and forth on crescents, and balances diamonds. (Ages 3–5)

REVIEWS: CL

Schultz, Lucy. *Farm Faces: A Book of Masks.* Illustrated by Ann Martin Larranaga. Norwalk, CT: innovativeKids, 2006.

Using simple rhymes, this book introduces children to chicks, sheep, pigs, and other farm animals. When the book is open, strategically positioned holes create a mask, which makes the book an interactive delight for young preschoolers. Other notable titles in the iBaby series include *Zoo Faces: A Book of Masks* and *Goodnight Faces: A Book of Masks.* (Ages 0–3)

Seder, Rufus Butler. *Swing!* Illustrated by the author. New York: Workman Publishing, 2008.

Through the wonder of Scanimation, an animation process that gives the illusion of movement, athletes seem to come alive as readers turn the pages. Children will be mesmerized as they watch young batters, runners, skaters, and swimmers in action. Seder's first book in Scanimation, *Gallop!* is also a notable title. (Ages 3–5)

REVIEWS: PW 09/22/08

Shapes. New York: Scholastic, 2007.

> As preschoolers identify and point to shapes on the left side of the book, they touch bumpy circles, smooth squares, scratchy triangles, and rough rectangles on the right. (Ages 0–2)

REVIEWS: CL

Shapiro, Arnold. *Triangles.* Illustrated by Bari Weissman. New York: Dial Books for Young Readers, 1992.

> When readers turn each page of this three-sided book, triangles in the form of trees, tents, mountains, and sails are formed. Other books in the Dial Playshapes Book series include *Circles* and *Squares.* (Ages 0–5)

REVIEWS: HBG 09/01/92; PW 04/13/92; KR 01/15/92

Shepherd, Jodie. *Ready for School.* Illustrated by Christopher Moroney. Pleasantville, NY: Reader's Digest Children's Books, 2006.

> With more than thirty flaps, readers can discover shapes, numbers, colors, action words, and healthy snacks with many of their favorite friends from *Sesame Street.* (Ages 4–5)

Sís, Peter. *Ballerina!* Illustrated by the author. New York: HarperFestival, 2005.

> Colors are explored as a young lover of dance leaps in red leotards, reaches in a yellow turban, dips in a white feather boa, and flutters in her green hat. The foldout finale reconnects the colors, costumes, and dances. *Ballerina!* is a celebration of color, dance, dreams, and imagination. (Ages 3–5)

REVIEWS: HBG 10/01/01; KR 07/20/01; BL 04/01/01; SLJ 04/01/01; PW 03/26/01; KR 03/15/01; CL

Sís, Peter. *Dinosaur!* Illustrated by the author. New York: Greenwillow Books, 2000.

> A young boy's imagination soars as a simple bath with a toy dinosaur turns into a prehistoric adventure with more than a dozen dinosaurs. Avid dinosaur fans will enjoy identifying the various species as they magically materialize from the tub. Front and back matter include names and illustrations of the dinosaurs featured in the book. (Ages 3–5)

REVIEWS: HBG 09/01/00; HBM 07/01/00; SLJ 06/01/00; BL 03/15/00; CL

Sís, Peter. *Fire Truck.* Illustrated by the author. New York: Greenwillow Books, 2004.

> Matt loves fire trucks. He is so fascinated by fire trucks that he dreams he became one. Youngsters will enjoy counting Matt's ladders, flashing lights, sirens, boots, and more. (Ages 3–5)
>
> REVIEWS: BL 09/15/98; HBM 09/01/98; SLJ 09/01/98; KR 08/01/98; CL

Slater, Dashka. *Baby Shoes.* Illustrated by Hiroe Nakata. New York: Bloomsbury Publishing, 2006.

> As a young boy enjoys a day of romping around town with his mother, his brand-new white shoes become "speckled, spotted, polka-dotted, puddle-stomping, rainbow-romping" by the end of the day. Both readers and listeners will love the rhymes and rhythm of this book as green grass, purple plums, and brown mud adorn the boy's shoes. (Ages 2–5)
>
> REVIEWS: HBG 10/01/06; SLJ 05/01/06; BL 05/01/06

Slaughter, Tom. *1, 2, 3.* Illustrated by the author. Plattsburgh, NY: Tundra Books, 2003.

> Bold, familiar objects like eyeglasses, buttons, fish, beach balls, and apple trees against solid backgrounds will make this counting book a favorite of a various range of preschoolers. For example, early counters may simply identify nine buildings; more advanced children may realize that each building also has nine windows. Because Tom Slaughter's art has been exhibited in modern galleries around the country, *1, 2, 3* also doubles as a book of art for young children. (Ages 2–5)
>
> REVIEWS: PW 12/12/05; PW 11/17/03; SLJ 11/01/03; CL

Watt, Fiona. *That's Not My Dolly* . . . Illustrated by Rachel Wells. Tulsa, OK: EDC Publishing, 2004.

> Spotted dresses, bumpy shoes, soft hats, and frizzy hair help young children find the desired doll—one with silky bows. Preschoolers of all ages will enjoy feeling the various textures as they turn each page. Other notable "touchy-feely" books by Watt include *That's Not My Fairy* . . ., *That's Not My Truck* . . ., and *That's Not My Mermaid* . . . (Ages 0–5)

Watt, Fiona. *Tie-a-Bow Book.* Illustrated by Stephen Cartwright. Tulsa, OK: EDC Publishing, 2002.

> Youngsters learn to tie, untie, and retie bows, strings, ribbons, and shoelaces in Millie's hair, Sam's sneakers, Poppy's apron, and Sam's present. (Ages 3–5)

Watt, Fiona. *Trucks.* Illustrated by Rachel Wells. Tulsa, OK: EDC Publishing, 2002.

> As readers turn each page, they will enjoy touching and feeling sparkly headlights, rough sides, zigzaggy dump truck beds, bumpy wheels, and spotted trailers. *Trucks* is the ideal book for all preschool truck lovers. (Ages 0–5)

Watt, Mélanie. *Shapes with Ocean Animals.* Illustrated by the author. Tonawanda, NY: Kids Can Press, 2005.

> Triangle fish, square stingrays, circle puffer fish, oval crabs, and other marine animals come alive in this small book of shapes. (Ages 1–2)
>
> REVIEWS: PW 04/25/05

Weiss, Ellen. *Feeling Happy.* Illustrated by Jason Jourdan. Worthington, OH: Brighter Minds Children's Publishing, 2006.

> Are you happy, grumpy, silly, angry, or shy? With the assistance of familiar animals, children explore these and other feelings by turning the wheel and matching faces with the feelings expressed by the book's characters. The back matter provides tips for becoming more aware of a child's feelings and how to talk to children about their emotions. (Ages 0–3)

Weiss, Ellen. *Fruit Salad.* Illustrated by Jason Jourdan. Worthington, OH: Brighter Minds Children's Publishing, 2006.

> As youngsters learn about nutrition and healthy foods, they can touch plastic grapes, apples, pears, and other fruits. As readers turn each page, the fruits disappear one by one and are placed in a bowl. The back matter includes nutrition tips and ideas for parents and child-care providers. (Ages 3–5)

Wood, Audrey. *The Napping House.* Illustrated by Don Wood. Orlando, FL: Red Wagon Books, 1996.

When readers enter the napping house, they are introduced to a cozy bed, a snoring granny, a dozing dog, a slumbering mouse, and other sleepy inhabitants. (Ages 3–5)

REVIEWS: HBG 10/01/01; HBG 09/01/96; BL 12/15/89; BL 09/01/86; CL

Wood, Jakki. *Moo, Moo, Brown Cow.* Illustrated by Rog Bonner. San Diego: Red Wagon Books, 1996.

A curious kitten visits Brown Cow, Yellow Goat, Blue Goose, Green Frog, and other mothers living on the farm, inquiring about their young. As readers count from one spotted calf to ten small fries (rainbow trout), they learn lessons of farm animals, including the sounds they make and names of their offspring. (Ages 1–5)

REVIEWS: HBG 09/01/92; SLJ 08/01/92; BL 06/15/92; KR 05/01/92; CL

Wormell, Christopher. *Teeth, Tales, and Tentacles: An Animal Counting Book.* Illustrated by the author. Philadelphia: Running Press Kids, 2006.

As older preschoolers count opossum babies, bear claws, caterpillar segments, rings on a lemur, and leopard rosettes, they will be enthralled by bold linocut illustrations of the twenty animals represented in this complex counting book. To encourage further exploration, miniature block prints and fascinating facts of the featured animals are found in the rear of the book. (Ages 4–5)

REVIEWS: HBG 04/01/05; BL 10/01/04; PW 08/23/04; KR 07/15/04; CL

Toy and Movable Books

Toy and Movable Books

These interactive books are visual, tactile, and often three-dimensional. As readers turn each new page, they are encouraged to peek through holes, lift flaps, touch, feel, pull, and manipulate objects. Toy and movable books allow preschoolers opportunities to become active parts of the stories they listen to and read.

Ackerman, Jill. *Peek-a-Zoo.* Illustrated by Fiona Land. New York: Scholastic, 2005.

> Variety is the key to this book as young readers are presented die-cuts, mirrors, flaps, shapes, colors, spatial concepts, sounds, touch, and textures. *The Crawly Caterpillar, Petting Farm*, and *The Tiny Tadpole* are other noteworthy interactive books in the Little Scholastic series. (Ages 0–3)
>
> *REVIEWS:* CL

Anderson, Sara Lee. *Numbers.* Illustrated by the author. New York: Handprint Books, 2007.

Sturdy, brightly colored graduated-cut pages teach readers to count from one to ten. The simple two-page illustrations dedicated to each number provide an array of objects to count. When preschoolers reach the number seven, for example, they discover seven dots, seven tigers, seven strips on each tiger, seven palm trees, and seven leaves on top of each palm tree. Constructed in a secure rectangular box, this book will be enjoyed by both beginning and experienced counters. (Ages 1–3)

REVIEWS: PW 11/05/07

Bataille, Marion. *ABC3D.* Designed by the author. New York: Roaring Book Press, 2008.

Bataille has created an imaginative three-dimensional pop-up book that readers of all ages will enjoy. The twenty-six letters pop, spin, and transform as readers turn each page. *ABC3D* is an innovative creation that children will cherish for many years. (Ages 1–5)

REVIEWS: BL 12/15/08; PW 08/18/08; CL

Bathtime Peekaboo! New York: DK Publishing, 2005.

Readers are encouraged to lift the flaps and feel scaly fish, bumpy starfish, smooth ducks, cuddly penguins, and squishy frogs as bath time approaches. (Ages 1–5)

REVIEWS: PW 08/08/05

Brown, Ruth. *The Tale of Two Mice.* Illustrated by the author. Cambridge, MA: Candlewick Press, 2008.

As two mice, Billy and Bo, search the mansion they live in for food, Bo is unaware of the danger that follows them as readers turn each page. Oversize pages of muted watercolor pictures, flaps, and a three-dimensional pop-up make this a suspenseful tale that children will want to read time and time again. (Ages 3–5)

REVIEWS: HBM 01/01/09; SLJ 01/01/09; BL 12/15/08; CL

Campbell, Rod. *Dear Zoo: A Lift-the-Flap Book.* Illustrated by the author. New York: Little Simon, 1999.

When a child writes to the zoo to request a pet, she must return animals that are too big, tall, fierce, grumpy, and naughty. Finally, the zoo sends her the perfect pet—a pet worth keeping. Different animals are revealed as youngsters lift each flap. (Ages 1–4)

REVIEWS: PW 04/25/05; CL

Carle, Eric. *My Very First Book of Colors.* Illustrated by the author. New York: Philomel Books, 2005.

In this toy and movable book, children are challenged to match pictures on the bottom half of the page with colors on the top half of the page. Levels of difficulty range from simple (brown shoes) to somewhat complex (a multicolored butterfly). (Ages 2–5)

REVIEWS: CL

Carle, Eric. *My Very First Book of Shapes.* Illustrated by the author. New York: Philomel Books, 2005.

In this toy and movable book, children are challenged to match pictures on the bottom half of the page with corresponding shapes on the top half of the page. Levels of difficulty range from simple circles and squares to somewhat complex shapes such as squiggles and crescents. (Ages 2–5)

REVIEWS: PW 04/25/05; CL

Carle, Eric. *Papa, Please Get the Moon for Me.* Illustrated by the author. New York: Simon & Schuster Books for Young Readers, 1986.

With the aid of a very long ladder, Monica's father gives her the moon to play with. Carle fans will appreciate his signature cut-paper collages and oversize foldout pages. (Ages 2–5)

REVIEWS: SLJ 08/01/86; PW 03/21/86; CL

Carle, Eric. *10 Little Rubber Ducks.* Illustrated by the author. New York: HarperCollins, 2005.

When the tenth lost rubber duck meets a live mother duck and her ducklings, he finds both a family and a home. As his new mother and siblings "quack" good night, readers will enjoy pressing a picture of the rubber duck, which allows him to "squeak" a response to his new family. (Ages 2–5)

REVIEWS: HBG 01/01/06; BL 05/01/05; PW 01/24/05; SLJ 01/01/05; CL

Carle, Eric. *The Very Busy Spider.* Illustrated by the author. New York: Philomel Books, 1984.

With the turn of each page, readers will see and feel the spider's silky web grow into a beautiful work of art as she diligently prepares to catch a pesky fly. (Ages 1–5)

REVIEWS: HBG 03/01/96; PW 08/14/1995; BL 12/15/89; CL

Carle, Eric. *The Very Clumsy Click Beetle.* Illustrated by the author. New York: Philomel Books, 1999.

With the encouragement of his friends, a young and awkward click beetle makes several attempts to flip through the air and land on his feet. When he finally succeeds and is praised by a wise old click beetle who is watching nearby, something amazing happens—an electronic chip embedded in the book makes the sound of a click beetle. (Ages 1–5)

REVIEWS: HBG 04/01/00; LJ 11/01/99; BL 10/01/99; PW 08/23/99; CL

Carle, Eric. *The Very Hungry Caterpillar.* Illustrated by the author. New York: Philomel Books, 1987.

Readers trace holes and lift flaps to follow a newly hatched caterpillar as he eats his way through pages filled with apples, plums, pickles, salamis, lollipops, and watermelons. Youngsters will enjoy watching the small caterpillar transform into a beautiful butterfly. (Ages 3–5)

REVIEWS: PW 11/03/03; HBG 03/01/95; CL

Carle, Eric. *The Very Lonely Firefly.* Illustrated by the author. New York: Philomel Books, 1995.

A lonely firefly encounters lightbulbs, candles, lanterns, fireworks, and other luminous things before meeting a group of fireflies. Carle's cut-paper collages and battery-powered flashing fireflies make this book a joy. (Ages 1–5)

REVIEWS: HBG 04/01/00; HBG 09/01/95; SLJ 08/01/95; PW 06/05/95; KR 06/01/95; BL 05/15/95; CL

Carle, Eric. *The Very Quiet Cricket.* Illustrated by the author. New York: Philomel Books, 1990.

> When a young cricket encounters locusts, spittlebugs, cicadas, bumblebees, and mosquitoes, who all greet him with their unique sounds, he tries to return their greeting by rubbing his wings together and chirping. Unfortunately, nothing happens. As he matures and meets a female cricket, he tries again. This time he makes the most beautiful sound the female cricket has ever heard. Readers will enjoy the battery-powered chirping sound the last page makes. (Ages 1–5)
>
> *REVIEWS:* HBG 09/01/97; HBG 03/01/91; SLJ 12/01/90; PW 11/19/90; PW 11/9/90; BL 10/01/90; CL

Carrier, Lark. *On Halloween.* Illustrated by the author. New York: HarperFestival, 1999.

> Die-cuts are used to create ghosts, jack-o-lanterns, skeletons, witches, bats, cats, and masks in this rhyming Halloween tale. (Ages 3–5)
>
> *REVIEWS:* CL

Carter, David. *Feely Bugs.* Illustrated by the author. New York: Little Simon, 1995.

> Carter has created a book filled with fuzzy, feathery, lacy, leathery, wrinkly, and crinkly bugs. Preschoolers will enjoy touching, feeling, and listening to the vast array of bug-eyed insects. (Ages 2–5)
>
> *REVIEWS:* PW 07/31/95

Carter, David A. *600 Black Spots.* Created by the author. New York: Little Simon, 2007.

> As readers turn each page of this pop-up book, an original kinetic sculpture, highlighted by black dots, appears. Branded as a "pop-up book for children of all ages," this collection of mesmerizing art is sure to be a book of choice for many years. *One Red Dot* is another noteworthy pop-up book by Carter. (Ages 3–5)

Carter, David, and Noelle Carter. *The Nutcracker.* Created by the authors. New York: Little Simon, 2000.

> Older preschoolers will enjoy this lavish pop-up adaptation of E. T. A. Hoffmann's original story. They will discover elaborate scenes unfolding as they lift flaps and pull tabs. (Ages 4–5)
>
> REVIEWS: PW 09/25/00; CL

Christian, Cheryl. *Where Does It Go?/¿Dónde va?* Photographed by Laura Dwight. New York: Star Bright Books, 2004.

> As readers turn pages and lift flaps, they will learn where diapers, shoes, hats, bears, and books belong. Additional titles in this bilingual series include *Where's the Puppy?/¿Dónde está el perrito? How Many?/¿Cuántos hay?* and *What Happens Next?/Y ahora, ¿qué pasará?* (Ages 0–3)
>
> REVIEWS: CL

Chwast, Seymour. *Mr. Merlin and the Turtle.* Illustrated by the author. New York: Greenwillow Books, 1996.

> Mr. Merlin uses his magical powers to turn his turtle into a bird when he and his wife become bored with their pet. When the bird becomes a nuisance, he changes it into another animal that becomes a greater nuisance. Readers will enjoy lifting flaps and discovering different animals as Mr. Merlin and his wife search for the perfect pet. (Ages 4–5)
>
> REVIEWS: HBG 03/01/97; SLJ 10/01/96/PW 06/24/96/KR 06/15/96

Crews, Donald. *Inside Freight Train.* Illustrated by the author. New York: HarperFestival, 2001.

> As readers explore engines, cattle cars, refrigerator cars, stock cars, and more, cardboard doors slide open, revealing the items, animals, and people commonly found on freight trains. (Ages 1–3)
>
> REVIEWS: HBG 10/01/01; PW 02/19/01; BL 12/15/00; CL

Curious George: Before and After. Boston: Houghton Mifflin, 2006.

> As readers turn pages and lift flaps, they will take an adventure with George as he experiences how it feels to be hungry and full, go up and down, and be dirty and clean. About more than simply opposites, this

colorful and sophisticated book in rhyme also teaches sequence and consequences. (Ages 1–3)

REVIEWS: CL

Dodds, Dayle Ann. *The Color Box.* Illustrated by Giles Laroche. Boston: Little, Brown, 1992.

Join Alexander, an adventurous monkey, as an ordinary-looking box leads him through worlds of color. As readers turn the pages, die-cuts remind them of previous journeys and provide glimpses of future explorations of black, yellow, orange, blue, red, green, purple, and white. Children will want to rediscover Alexander's travels again and again. (Ages 2–5)

REVIEWS: HBG 09/01/92; SLJ 06/01/92; BL 05/01/92; KR 03/15/92

Ehlert, Lois. *Color Zoo.* Illustrated by the author. New York: J. B. Lippincott, 1989.

Meticulously arranged die-cuts use geometric shapes to bring tigers, monkeys, lions, snakes, and other animals alive. Readers will be captivated as brightly colored faces of animals transform as squares, hexagons, circles, diamonds, and hearts are added and removed. *Color Zoo* is an ideal book for teaching colors, shapes, and animal recognition. An additional notable book by Ehlert that is similar in style is *Color Farm.* (Ages 1–5)

REVIEWS: HBG 09/01/97; BL 03/15/90; BL 05/15/89; SLJ 04/01/89; CL

Ehlert, Lois. *Hands.* Illustrated by the author. New York: Harcourt Brace, 1997.

In this glove-shaped book, Ehlert describes how she and her parents used their hands and tools during her childhood. As her father built things in his workshop and her mother made crafts and clothes, the author would enjoy crafting and painting. Gardening was something they all enjoyed doing. Readers will enjoy the superior design of this book, including the flaps, foldout pages, and gloves. (Ages 4–5)

REVIEWS: HBG 03/01/98; SLJ 12/01/97; BL 11/15/97; KR 07/15/97; PW 06/30/97

Ehlert, Lois. *In My World.* Illustrated by the author. New York: Harcourt, 2002.

Ehlert uses die-cut shapes and colors to create incredible images of things she enjoys. Three-dimensional overlaying pages of bugs, frogs, stones, fish, fruit, and rain magically materialize on each page. The back matter includes a rebus poem that reintroduces readers to many of the book's images. (Ages 3–5)

REVIEWS: PW 01/09/06; HBG 10/01/02; HBM 07/01/02; SLJ 05/01/02; BL 05/01/02; KR 03/01/02; PW 02/18/02; CL

Emberley, Ed. *Go Away, Big Green Monster!* Illustrated by the author. New York: Little, Brown, 1992.

Die-cuts create a big green monster with two yellow eyes, a red mouth with sharp white teeth, and purple hair. Too scary? Simply continue turning the pages, and each scary feature disappears as quickly as it appeared. Readers will not fear this monster because he returns only when the child wants him to. Emberley's work is the ideal for helping preschoolers understand and overcome their fears. (Ages 1–5)

REVIEWS: PW 10/10/05; HBG 09/01/93; SLJ 07/01/93; BL 04/15/93; BL 04/01/93; PW 03/29/93; KR 03/15/93; CL

Emma Treehouse Ltd. *My Pets.* Illustrated by Caroline Davis. Wilton, CT: Tiger Tales, 2007.

With the aid of chunky, sturdy tabs, young preschoolers lift flaps to lend a hand as a girl searches for her pet rabbit, cat, and dog. Other notable titles in the Easy Flaps series include *My Babies*, *My Friends*, and *My Toys*. (Ages 0–2)

REVIEWS: CL

Ernst, Lisa Campbell. *The Turn-Around, Upside-Down Alphabet Book.* Illustrated by the author. New York: Simon & Schuster Books for Young Readers, 2004.

As the reader turns the book in various directions, letters transform into different objects. The letter *E* becomes an electric plug, the number three, and candles on a birthday cake, while the letter *U* becomes a magnet, a droopy mustache, and a hot dog on a bun. Older preschoolers will be particularly fond of Ernst's abstract illustrations. (Ages 3–5)

REVIEWS: HBG 04/01/05; SLJ 08/01/04; HBM 07/01/04; PW 06/14/04; BL 06/01/04; CL

Fowler, Richard. *There's a Mouse about the House.* Illustrated by the author. Tulsa: EDC Publishing, 1983.

> Follow the dotted line as a hungry gray mouse searches the house for a bite to eat. Readers slide a cardboard mouse through slots as he darts between floorboards, scampers under pantry doors, dashes out of empty boxes of cereal, climbs stairs, runs under beds, scurries up nightshirts, and more. Children will want to read the book again. (Ages 3–5)

Fry, Sonali. *My Busy Day.* Photographed by Ken Karp Photography. New York: Simon & Schuster Children's Publishing, 2006.

> As the children in the book get dressed, eat, play with toys, visit the park, and prepare for bed, readers can interact with them by tying ribbons on dresses, touching shiny boots, seeing their reflections in silverware, and rubbing soft towels. The sturdy handle makes this a book toddlers will enjoy carrying from place to place. *My Busy Day* is one of the notable titles in Baby Nick Jr.'s Curious Buddies series. (Ages 1–3)
>
> REVIEWS: CL

Gerstein, Mordicai. *Roll Over!* Illustrated by the author. New York: Crown Publishers, 1984.

> Sister Seal, Uncle Unicorn, Grandma Goose, Cousin Camel, and other animals crowd a young boy's bed. As the boy demands that each person on the end roll over, they fall out one by one until only the boy is left. The foldout pages add suspense to the familiar children's rhyme, since readers do not know who will fall out until they lift the flap. (Ages 3–5)

Guettier, Bénédicte. *In the Jungle . . .* Illustrated by the author. La Jolla, CA: Kane/Miller Book Publishers, 2002.

> By placing their faces in large cutout circles, readers instantly transform into bears, elephants, crocodiles, monkeys, and other familiar zoo animals. (Ages 0–3)
>
> REVIEWS: PW 10/21/02; CL

Gunzi, Christiane. *Furry Kittens.* Photographed by the author. Hauppauge, NY: Barron's Educational Series, 2005.

Kittens come to life as readers stoke their soft fur, feel their rough tongues, touch their soft cushions, and more. Other titles in the Feels Real series include *Cuddly Puppies*, *On the Farm*, *Under the Sea*, *In the Jungle*, and *Little Ponies*. (Ages 1–4)

Hill, Eric. *Spot Sleeps Over.* Illustrated by the author. New York: G. P. Putnam's Sons, 1990.

The lift-the-flap adventure begins as Spot packs for his sleepover with his next-door neighbor Steve. Readers must wait until they lift the last flap to discover what is in the pink bag. (Ages 1–3)

REVIEWS: HBG 03/01/91; SLJ 03/01/91; PW 08/31/90

Huddleston, Ruth, and Wendy Madgwick. *Time for Bed.* Illustrated by Tony Linsell. Brookfield, CT: Copper Beech Books, 1996.

Benny Bear's birthday party is filled with cake, friends, and games. As bedtime arrives and guests fall asleep one by one, readers are encouraged to place each press-out character in his or her proper bed. This interactive bedtime story concludes with Mommy Bear wishing Benny and all of his friends a final goodnight. (Ages 1–5)

Johnson, Richard. *Look at Me in Funny Clothes!* Illustrated by Martin Chatterton. Cambridge, MA: Candlewick Press, 1994.

In this cleverly designed book, readers can try on clothes and become deep-sea divers, superheroes, and skeletons by simply turning pages. (Ages 3–5)

Katz, Karen. *What Does Baby Say?* Illustrated by the author. New York: Little Simon, 2004.

In addition to learning that happy babies say "goo-goo!" and sad babies say "boo-hoo!" this straightforward lift-the-flap book demonstrates sounds of hungry, cuddly, busy, cranky, and sleepy babies. (Ages 1–5)

REVIEWS: CL

Klausmeier, Jesse. *Open This Little Book.* Illustrated by Suzy Lee. San Francisco: Chronicle Books, 2013.

Preschoolers learn primary colors as ladybugs, frogs, rabbits, and bears open, read, and close books in shades of red, green, orange, yellow, and blue. With each page the books become smaller, but they gradually return to their original size. Youngsters will enjoy the innovative concept of this simple, charming book. (Ages 3–5)

REVIEWS: KR 01/15/13; PW 01/07/13

Laden, Nina. *Peek-a-Who?* Illustrated by the author. San Francisco: Chronicle Books, 2000.

Simple rhyming text and die-cut windows make this the ideal guessing book for preschool children. The mirrored end page, appropriately captioned, "Peek a YOU!" is sure to delight young readers again and again. (Ages 0–2)

REVIEWS: SLJ 07/01/00

Leslie, Amanda. *Play, Puppy, Play.* Illustrated by the author. Cambridge, MA: Candlewick Press, 1992.

When readers place their fingers through the open spaces strategically created on each page, tails, trunks, wings, fins, and legs of dogs, elephants, ducks, fish, and caterpillars come to life. *Play, Kitten, Play* is another notable title in the Ten Animal Fingerwiggles series. (Ages 1–3)

REVIEWS: HBG 03/01/93; BL 11/15/92

McGuire, Leslie. *Brush Your Teeth Please.* Illustrated by Jean Pidgeon. Pleasantville, NY: Reader's Digest Children's Book, 1993.

This pop-up book is filled with hygiene-conscious bears, chimps, hippos, lions, and sharks who encourage young children to brush and floss their teeth properly. The back matter includes an embedded mirror so readers can see their very own smiles. (Ages 2–5)

Morrow, Tara Jaye. *Mommy Loves Her Baby/Daddy Loves His Baby.* Illustrated by Tiphanie Beeke. New York: HarperCollins Publishers, 2003.

The story begins with a mother describing the many ways she loves her son. Midway through the book, the reader is instructed to flip over the book. At this point, father tells the boy how much he loves him. Preschoolers will understand the meaning of security and love after hearing this tender story. (Ages 1–3)

REVIEWS: HBG 10/01/03; SLJ 07/01/03; HBM 05/01/03; KR 03/15/03; PW 03/03/03; CL

My First Counting (Touch and Feel). New York: DK Publishing, 2005.

As readers count in the garden, in a traffic jam, while matching pairs, in art class, and at a teddy bear picnic, they have opportunities to touch and feel shiny beetles, wooly sheep, sparkly socks, sticky paint, and shiny party hats. (Ages 1–5)

Newcome, Zita. *Toddlerobics: Fun Action Rhymes.* Illustrated by the author. Cambridge, MA: Candlewick Press, 2002.

Nursery rhymes like "Row, Row, Row Your Boat," "Pat-a-Cake," "This Is the Way the Lady Rides," and "If You're Happy and You Know It" come alive as readers pull tabs and turn wheels in this fun-filled pop-up book. (Ages 3–5)

REVIEWS: PW 10/28/02; CL

No Potty! Yes, Potty! Illustrated by Emily Bolam. New York: Sterling Publishing, 2006.

In this humorous lift-the-flap introduction to potty training, readers will laugh as they see monkeys, bears, elephants, and other animals attempting to use potties. Young Max finally shows children how to properly use the potty. *Go, Girl! Go Potty!* is the companion book for girls. (Ages 1–3)

Numbers. Illustrated by Fiona Land. New York: Ladybird Books, 2008.

As young children touch and feel soft caterpillars, bumpy frogs, furry cats, and more, they also learn to count from one to five. (Ages 0–2)

Pandell, Karen. *Animal Action ABC.* Photographed by Art Wolfe and Nancy Sheehan. New York: Dutton Children's Books, 1996.

This book encourages movement and exercise as children arch their backs and stretch like humpback whales, charge their prey like jaguars, kick like kangaroos, wrestle like two tigers, and zap insects with their tongues like chameleons. Preschoolers of all ages will enjoy imitating the children and animals photographed on the oversize pages, and older children will appreciate the nature notes found in the back matter. (Ages 2–5)

REVIEWS: PW 05/26/03; HBG 03/01/97; BL 11/15/96; PW 10/14/96; KR 09/15/96

Peek-a-Boo What? Illustrated by Elliot Kreloff. New York: Begin Smart, 2009.

Simple rhymes; die-cut holes; foldout pages; and illustrations of dogs, fish, socks, and cows combine to make this an interactive treat for young readers. (Ages 1–2)

REVIEWS: BL 12/01/09

Petty, Colin. *Colors.* Illustrated by the author. Hauppauge, NY: Barron's Educational Series, 2005.

As children place a finger in a small hole and slide it to the left or right, the answer to the question, "What color?" appears in a cutout box on the corresponding page. As one of the four titles in the Concept Sliders series, *Colors* is an entertaining way to introduce basic colors to youngsters. (Ages 1–3)

REVIEWS: PW 08/28/06; CL

Pinto, Sara. *The Alphabet Room.* Illustrated by the author. New York: Bloomsbury, 2003.

As readers turn each page, objects representing each letter of the alphabet are announced and creatively placed in a room. Each time a door within a room is opened, a new, delightful scene is revealed. Intrigue and excitement build as more and more objects are added and the scenes become more outrageous. This charming cumulative book is both simple and complex, which will allow it to be a child's favorite for many years. (Ages 0–5)

REVIEWS: BL 02/01/04; PW 10/27/03; CL

Powers, Amelia. *Giant Pop-Out Shapes.* San Francisco: Chronicle Books, 2007.

Learning about circles, squares, triangles, ovals, stars, and hearts is easy when buttons, crackers, slices of pizza, and other everyday items are teaching aids. As pages unfold, revealing giant pop-out shapes, readers receive additional surprises. (Ages 1–4)

REVIEWS: SLJ 01/01/08; PW 08/27/07

Rey, Margret, and H. A. Rey. *Curious George at the Zoo: A Touch and Feel Book.* Illustrated by the authors. Boston: Houghton Mifflin Company, 2007.

Curious George fans will enjoy spending a day at the zoo with the playful monkey. Readers will be able to touch and feel a penguin's thick coat, smooth water, a rhino's rough skin, a bumpy basket, and more. (Ages 0–3)

Saltzberg, Barney. *Animal Kisses.* Illustrated by the author. San Diego: Red Wagon Books, 2000.

After experiencing kisses from scratchy cats, velvety cows, squeaky pigs, and more, readers must decide what kind of kisses they like best. This book is filled with delightful illustrations, textures, and sounds. (Ages 1–3)

Saltzberg, Barney. *Beautiful Oops!* Illustrated by the author. New York: Workman Publishing, 2010.

While examining torn pages, spills, bent pages, smudges and smears, holes, and more, readers will see the beauty and creative opportunities that mistakes and imperfections offer. Preschoolers will enjoy the bright, bold illustrations as they lift flaps and as holes spiral toward them. (Ages 3–5)

REVIEWS: KR 12/01/10; PW 08/23/10; CL

Sawyer, Parker K. *Potty Time!* Illustrated by Christopher Moroney. New York: Random House, 2006.

Join Grover and many of his Sesame Street friends as they explore and share their experiences with a large white porcelain fixture in the bathroom—the toilet. On the final page of the book, children can share in Grover's excitement of using the potty for the first time by moving the tab on the toilet to simulate flushing. (Ages 2–3)

REVIEWS: CL

Schultz, Lucy. *Farm Faces: A Book of Masks.* Illustrated by Ann Martin Larranaga. Norwalk, CT: innovativeKids, 2006.

Using simple rhymes, this book introduces children to chicks, sheep, pigs, and other farm animals. When the book is open, strategically positioned holes create a mask, which makes the book an interactive delight for young preschoolers. Other notable titles in the iBaby series include *Zoo Faces: A Book of Masks* and *Goodnight Faces: A Book of Masks.* (Ages 0–3)

Schwarz, Viviane. *There Are Cats in This Book.* Illustrated by the author. Cambridge, MA: Candlewick Press, 2008.

> Readers will enjoy meeting and playing with Moonpie, Tiny, and André in this interactive story. In addition to lifting flaps to reveal the next escapade, readers are encouraged to throw yarn, return to previous pages, participate in a pillow fight, and blow on pages to dry off the wet felines. Schwarz's friendly cats can also be found in *There Are No Cats in This Book.* (Ages 2–4)
>
> REVIEWS: SLJ 12/01/08; PW 09/29/08; CL

Seder, Rufus Butler. *Swing!* Illustrated by the author. New York: Workman Publishing, 2008.

> Through the wonder of Scanimation, an animation process that gives the illusion of movement, athletes seem to come alive as readers turn the pages. Children will be mesmerized as they watch young batters, runners, skaters, and swimmers in action. Seder's first book in Scanimation, *Gallop!*, is also a notable title. (Ages 3–5)
>
> REVIEWS: PW 09/22/08

Seeger, Laura Vaccaro. *First the Egg.* Illustrated by the author. New Milford, CT: Roaring Brook Press, 2007.

> Seeger uses small, subtle die-cuts and textured illustrations to demonstrate sequencing to preschool children. In addition to learning that chickens were once eggs, readers discover that frogs were once tadpoles, that flowers grow from seeds, and that even stories and pictures begin as words and paint. As this skillful story comes to a close, an age-old question resurfaces—which came first, the chicken or the egg? (Ages 3–5)
>
> REVIEWS: BL 02/01/08; HBM 11/01/07; SLJ 11/01/07; KR 09/01/07; PW 08/20/07; CL

Seeger, Laura Vaccaro. *The Hidden Alphabet.* Illustrated by the author. Brookfield, CT: Roaring Brook Press, 2003.

> Pictures surrounded by a black mat and representing letters of the alphabet appear on each page of this book. When readers raise the flaps, each object characterized in this spectacular book transforms into a bold and distinct letter. Older preschoolers will find the unconventional shapes of the letters both challenging and exciting. (Ages 4–5)
>
> REVIEWS: SLJ 10/01/04; HBG 04/01/04; BL 02/01/04; HB 01/01/04; SLJ 11/01/03; PW 09/08/03; KR 08/15/03; CL

Seeger, Laura Vaccaro. *Lemons Are Not Red.* Illustrated by the author. Brookfield, CT: Roaring Book Press, 2004.

Through the use of simple and detailed die-cuts, red lemons magically turn yellow, gray flamingos enchantingly become pink, and blue grass grows to be green. Children will find humor in the initial unnatural colors of well-known items and will be intrigued as the objects materialize into their customary hues. The night fades to black with the final words of the book, "Good night," making Vaccaro's book an ideal bedtime read. (Ages 2–5)

REVIEWS: HBG 04/01/05; HBM 01/01/05; BL 01/01/05; PW 11/15/04; KR 10/01/04; CL

Shapes. New York: Scholastic, 2007.

As preschoolers identify and point to shapes on the left side of the book, they touch bumpy circles, smooth squares, scratchy triangles, and rough rectangles on the right. (Ages 0–2)

Sharratt, Nick. *Ketchup on Your Cornflakes?* Illustrated by the author. New York: Cartwheel Books, 1997.

Wacky questions like "Do you like ketchup in your ginger ale?" and "Do you like ice cream on your toes?" will make children amusingly scream, "No!" as they turn each split, sturdy page of this spiral-bound book. They will yell, "Yes!" when color-coded pages match, revealing questions such as "Do you like ice cream on your apple pie?" The bright, simple illustrations of this "wacky" mix-and-match book are sure to bring smiles to young faces. (Ages 3–5)

REVIEWS: HBG 09/01/97; KR 05/01/97

Shea, Susan A. *Do You Know Which Ones Will Grow?* Illustrated by Tom Slaughter. Maplewood, NJ: Blue Apple Books, 2011.

As preschoolers lift flaps and peep through die-cuts, they learn the difference between things that grow and things that remain the way they were initially made. This story in rhyme illustrates that although cubs, calves, piglets, and kits grown up to become bears, cows, pigs, and foxes, cars, stools, caps, and shovels do not grow and become trucks, chairs, hats, and plows. Children will enjoy answering yes or no to the questions presented to them. (Ages 4–5)

REVIEWS: HBG 10/01/11; SLJ 06/01/11; KR 04/01/11; PW 03/28/11; CL

Slater, Dashka. *Baby Shoes.* Illustrated by Hiroe Nakata. New York: Bloomsbury Publishing, 2006.

> As a young boy enjoys a day of romping around town with his mother, his brand-new white shoes become "speckled, spotted, polka-dotted, puddle-stomping, rainbow-romping" by the end of the day. Both readers and listeners will love the rhymes and rhythm of this book as green grass, purple plums, and brown mud adorn the boy's shoes. (Ages 2–5)
>
> REVIEWS: HBG 10/01/06; SLJ 05/01/06; BL 05/01/06

Taback, Simms. *Do You Have a Tail?* Illustrated by the author. Maplewood, NJ: Blue Apple Books, 2007.

> A little mouse asks a zebra, goat, mouse, and seal if they have body parts such as noses, eyes, ears, and whiskers. The questioning mouse, a finger puppet attached to this board book, makes Taback's tale book both unique and interactive. (Ages 1–5)
>
> REVIEWS: PW 07/23/07; CL

Taback, Simms. *Where Is My Friend?* Illustrated by the author. Maplewood, NJ: Blue Apple Books, 2006.

> Elephant, Zebra, Seal, and other zoo animals search for their friends. As readers lift flaps and find the friends, the animals' sad faces instantly change to expressions of glee. (Ages 2–5)
>
> REVIEWS: PW 08/28/06

Tabby, Abigail. *Snap! Button! Zip!* Illustrated by Christopher Moroney. New York: Random House, 2003.

> Preschoolers learn to dress themselves as they practice snapping pants, buttoning sweaters, and zipping jackets with their friend Zoe from *Sesame Street*. (Ages 2–3)

Tildes, Phyllis Limbacher. *Eye Guess: A Foldout Guessing Game.* Watertown, MA: Charlesbridge, 2005.

> Children will be fascinated by each close-up illustration of an animal accompanied by several clues to assist them in solving a mystery. As pages unfold, ducks, turtles, raccoons, owls, and other amazing animals are revealed. (Ages 4–5)
>
> REVIEWS: HBG 01/01/06; BL 09/01/05; CL

Tullet, Hervé. *Press Here.* Illustrated by the author. San Francisco: Chronicle Books, 2011.

As they read this colorful and charming text, children are encouraged to press, rub, and blow on dots, shake and tilt the book, and clap as instructed. To enjoy the book to its fullest, however, preschoolers should have mastered counting skills and be able to recognize basic colors. *Press Here* is an excellent book for teaching children to listen and follow directions. (Ages 3–5)

REVIEWS: HBG 10/01/11; HBM 07/01/11; SLJ 04/01/11; KR 03/01/11; PW 01/31/11; CL

Tyler, Jenny. *Animal Hide-and-Seek.* Illustrated by Stephen Cartwright. Tulsa, OK: EDC Publishing, 2003.

As readers count and lift flaps to play hide-and-seek with animals and children, they will feel fur, wool, shiny pales, bowls of grain, and blue jeans. (Ages 1–5)

REVIEWS: CL

Van Fleet, Matthew. *One Yellow Lion.* Illustrated by the author. New York: Dial Books for Young Readers, 1992.

In addition to learning their colors, preschoolers will practice counting from one to ten as each page folds out to reveal lions, squirrels, lizards, alligators, and more. The book ends with a gleeful five-page foldout of all the animals enjoying a day at the shore. (Ages 1–5)

REVIEWS: SLJ 09/01/92; PW 05/25/92; CL

Warner, Sharon, and Sarah Forss. *Alphabeasties and Other Amazing Types.* Illustrated by the authors. Maplewood, NJ: Blue Apple Books, 2009.

Letters in various typefaces outline animals in this clever and innovative alphabet book. From the brilliant pullout pages of alligators and giraffes to the one-page interpretations of camels and walruses, this amazing book is a celebration of animals and of both the beauty and the power of typefaces. (Ages 4–5)

REVIEWS: PW 10/26/09; SLJ 10/01/09

Watt, Fiona. *That's Not My Dolly . . .* Illustrated by Rachel Wells. Tulsa: EDC Publishing, 2004.

> Spotted dresses, bumpy shoes, soft hats, and frizzy hair help young children find the desired doll—one with silky bows. Preschoolers of all ages will enjoy feeling the various textures as they turn each page. Other notable "touchy-feely" books by Watt include *That's Not My Fairy . . .*, *That's Not My Truck . . .*, and *That's Not My Mermaid . . .* (Ages 0–5)

Watt, Fiona. *Tie-a-Bow Book.* Illustrated by Stephen Cartwright. Tulsa: EDC Publishing, 2002.

> Youngsters learn to tie, untie, and retie bows, strings, ribbons, and shoelaces in Millie's hair, Sam's sneakers, Poppy's apron, and Sam's present. (Ages 3–5)

Watt, Fiona. *Trucks.* Illustrated by Rachel Wells. Tulsa, OK: EDC Publishing, 2002.

> As readers turn each page, they will enjoy touching and feeling sparkly headlights, rough sides, zigzaggy dump truck beds, bumpy wheels, and spotted trailers. *Trucks* is the ideal book for all preschool truck lovers. (Ages 0–5)

Weiss, Ellen. *Feeling Happy.* Illustrated by Jason Jourdan. Worthington, OH: Brighter Minds Children's Publishing, 2006.

> Are you happy, grumpy, silly, angry, or shy? With the assistance of familiar animals, children explore these and other feelings by turning the wheel and matching faces with the feelings expressed by the book's characters. The back matter provides tips for becoming more aware of a child's feelings and how to talk to children about their emotions. (Ages 0–3)

Weiss, Ellen. *Fruit Salad.* Illustrated by Jason Jourdan. Worthington, OH: Brighter Minds Children's Publishing, 2006.

> As youngsters learn about nutrition and healthy foods, they can touch plastic grapes, apples, pears, and other fruits. As readers turn each page, the fruits disappear one by one and are placed in a bowl. The back matter includes nutrition tips and ideas for parents and child-care providers. (Ages 3–5)
>
> *REVIEWS:* CL

Wilson-Max, Ken. *Little Green Tow Truck.* Illustrated by the author. New York: Cartwheel Books, 1997.

In this interactive venture, readers will start the engine, shift gears, open the glove compartment, hook up a car, and more as the small green tow truck responds to a call from a car stranded on the main highway. (Ages 3–5)

REVIEWS: HBG 09/01/97; CL

Zelinsky, Paul O. *Knick-Knack Paddywhack!* Illustrated by the author. New York: Dutton Children's Books, 2002.

In this skillfully crafted toy and movable adaptation of the well-known folk song, readers of all ages will marvel at the animation experienced through pulling tabs, lifting and turning flaps, and spinning wheels. Children will count, laugh, clap, and sing for hours as these old men come rolling home. (Ages 2–5)

REVIEWS: HBG 04/01/03; HBM 01/01/03; SLJ 12/01/02; BL 11/01/02; KR 08/15/02; PW 08/12/02; CL

Zelinsky, Paul O. *The Wheels on the Bus.* Illustrated by the author. New York: Dutton Children's Books, 1990.

This traditional children's song comes to life as wheels turn, doors open and shut, people step in and out, windows slide up and down, wipers swish, and more. The design is brilliant, and for those wishing to add piano or guitar, music and lyrics are printed on the back cover. (Ages 2–5)

REVIEWS: HBG 03/01/91; SLJ 10/01/90; PW 09/28/90

Ziefert, Harriet. *Where Is Humpty Dumpty?* Illustrated by Laura Rader. New York: Sterling Publishing, 2004.

As readers turn the sturdy, split pages of this flip-and-read book, rhymes and illustrations reveal five Mother Goose favorites, including "Hey Diddle Diddle" and "Humpty Dumpty." Another notable flip-and-read book is *What Happened to Jack and Jill?* (Ages 3–5)

CHAPTER 8

Resources for Building a Core Collection

Early Literacy

Arnold, Renea. 2003. "Public Libraries and Early Literacy: Raising a Reader." *American Libraries* 34: 48–51.

Between the Lions. 2010. *Wild about Group Time: Simply Literacy Plans for Preschool.* Silver Spring, MD: Gryphon House.

———. 2010. *Wild about Literacy: Fun Activities for Preschool.* Silver Spring, MD: Gryphon House.

Christie, James F., Billie Jean Enz, and Carol Vukelich. 2011. *Teaching Language and Literacy: Preschool through the Elementary Grades.* Boston: Pearson.

Court, Joy. 2011. *Read to Succeed: Strategies to Engage Children and Young People in Reading for Pleasure.* London: Facet.

Diamant-Cohen, Betsy, and Saroj Nadkarni Ghoting. 2010. *The Early Literacy Kit: A Handbook and Tip Cards.* Chicago: American Library Association.

Ernst, Linda L. 2012. *The Essential Lapsit Guide.* New York: Neal-Schuman Publishers.

Feinberg, Sandra, Barbara Jordan, Kathleen Deerr, Marcellina Byrne, and Lisa G. Kropp. 2007. *The Family-Centered Library Handbook.* New York: Neal-Schuman Publishers.

Galda, Lee, Lawrence R. Sipe, Lauren A. Liang, and Bernice E. Cullinan. 2014. *Literature and the Child.* OH: Cengage Learning.

Gambrell, Linda B., Lesley Mandel Morrow, and Michael Pressley, eds. 2007.

Best Practices in Literacy Instruction. New York: Guilford Press.

Giorgis, Cyndi, and Joan I. Glazer. 2013. *Literature for Young Children: Supporting Emergent Literacy, Ages 0–8*. Boston: Pearson.

Griffith, Priscilla L. 2008. *Literacy for Young Children: A Guide for Early Childhood Educators*. Thousand Oaks, CA: Corwin Press.

Hansen, Harlan S., and Ruth M. Hansen. 2010. *Lessons for Literacy: Promoting Preschool Success*. St. Paul, MN: Redleaf Press.

Jay, Hilda L., and M. Ellen Jay. 2000. *250+ Activities and Ideas for Developing Literacy Skills*. New York: Neal-Schuman Publishers.

Justice, Laura M., and Carol Vukelich, eds. 2008. *Achieving Excellence in Preschool Literacy Instruction*. New York: Guilford Press.

Lee, Kyunghwa, and Mark D. Vagle. 2012. *Developmentalism in Early Childhood and Middle Grades Education: Critical Conversations on Readiness and Responsiveness*. New York: Palgrave Macmillan.

Lybolt, John. 2007. *Building Language throughout the Year: The Preschool Early Literacy Curriculum*. Baltimore: Paul H. Brookes Publishing.

McKenna, Michael C., Sharon Walpole, and Kristin Conradi, eds. 2010. *Promoting Early Reading: Research, Resources, and Best Practices*. New York: Guilford Press.

Nevills, Pamela, and Patricia Wolfe. 2009. *Building the Reading Brain, PreK–3*. Thousand Oaks, CA: Corwin Press.

Notari-Syverson, Angela, Rollanda E. O'Connor, and Patricia F. Vadasy. 2007. *Ladders to Literacy: A Preschool Activity Book*. Baltimore: Paul H. Brookes Publishing.

Petersen, Sandra H., and Donna S. Wittmer. 2012. *Endless Opportunities for Infant and Toddler Curriculum: A Relationship-Based Approach*. Boston: Pearson.

Pica, Rae. 2007. *Jump into Literacy: Active Learning for Preschool Children*. Beltsville, MD: Gryphon House.

Soderman, Anne Keil, and Patricia Farrell. 2008. *Creating Literacy-Rich Preschools and Kindergartens*. Boston: Pearson.

Stoltz, Dorothy, Elaine M. Czarnecki, and Connie Wilson. 2012. *Every Child Ready for School: Helping Adults Inspire Young Children to Learn*. Chicago: American Library Association.

Temple, Charles A., Donna Ogle, Alan N. Crawford, and Penny Freppon. 2005. *All Children Read: Teaching for Literacy in Today's Diverse Classroom*. Boston: Pearson.

Totten, Kathryn. 2009. *Family Literacy Storytimes: Readymade Storytimes Suitable for the Whole Family*. New York: Neal-Schuman Publishers.

US Department of Education. 2005. *Helping Your Child Become a Reader*. Jessup, MD: Education Publications Center.

Vukelich, Carol, and James Christie. 2009. *Building a Foundation for Preschool Literacy: Effective Instruction for Children's Reading and Writing Development*. Newark, DE: International Reading Association.

Weiss, Laura B. 2006. "Brooklyn Reads to Babies." *School Library Journal* 52: 22.

Fingerplays and Action Rhymes

Brown, Marc. 1980. *Finger Rhymes*. New York: E. P. Dutton.

Brown, Marc. 1988. *Party Rhymes*. New York: E. P. Dutton.

Cole, Joanna, and Stephanie Calmenson. 1991. *The Eentsy, Weentsy Spider: Fingerplays and Action Rhymes*. New York: Morrow Junior Books.

———. 1992. *Pat-a-Cake and Other Play Rhymes*. New York: Morrow Junior Books.

Defty, Jeff. 1992. *Creative Fingerplays and Action Rhymes: An Index and Guide to Their Use*. Phoenix: Oryx Press.

Schiller, Pam, and Thomas Moore. 2004. *Do You Know the Muffin Man? An Essential Preschool Literacy Resource*. Beltsville, MD: Gryphon House.

Yolen, Jane. 1989. *The Lap-Time Song and Play Book*. San Diego: Harcourt Brace Jovanovich.

Review Sources

Journals

Booklist. Chicago: American Library Association.

Bulletin of the Center for Children's Books. Baltimore: Johns Hopkins University Press.

Horn Book Guide to Children's and Young Adult Books. Boston: Horn Book.

Horn Book Magazine: Recommending Books for Children and Young Adults. Boston: Horn Book.

Kirkus Reviews. Austin: Kirkus Media.

Library Journal. New York: Library Journal.

New York Times Book Review. New York: New York Times Company.

Publisher's Weekly: The International News Magazine of Book Publishing. New York: PWxyz.

Quill and Quire: Canada's Magazine of Book News and Reviews. Toronto: St. Joseph Media.

School Library Journal: The World's Largest Reviewer of Books, Multimedia, and Technology for Children and Teens. New York: Media Source.

Databases

Children's Literature. www.childrenslit.com.

Children's Literature Comprehensive Database. www.clcd.com.

Booklists

Association for Library Services to Children. 2014. "Children's Notable Lists." www.ala.org/alsc/awardsgrants/notalists.

Barr, Catherine, and John T. Gillespie. 2010. *Best Books for Children: Preschool through Grade 6.* Westport, CT: Libraries Unlimited.

Children's Literature Comprehensive Database. 2014. www.clcd.com.

Children's Literature Web Guide. 2014. "Lots of Lists." http://people.ucalgary .ca/~dkbrown/lists.html.

Cianciolo, Patricia J. 1997. *Picture Books for Children.* Chicago: American Library Association.

———. 2000. *Informational Picture Books for Children.* Chicago: American Library Association.

Darigan, Daniel L., Michael O. Tunnell, and James S. Jacobs. 2002. *Children's Literature: Engaging Teachers and Children in Good Books.* Upper Saddle River, NJ: Merrill/Prentice Hall.

Donavin, Denise Perry, ed. 1992. *American Library Association Best of the Best for Children: Books, Magazines, Videos, Audio, Software, Toys, Travel.* New York: Random House.

Dreyer, Sharon Spredemann. 1992. *The Best of Bookfinder: A Guide to Children's Literature about Interests and Concerns of Youth Aged 2–18.* Circle Pines, MN: American Guidance Service.

Freeman, Judy. 1990. *Books Kids Will Sit Still For: The Complete Read-Aloud Guide*. New York: R. R. Bowker.

———. 1995. *More Books Kids Will Sit Still For: A Read-Aloud Guide*. New Providence, NJ: R. R. Bowker.

———. 2006. *Books Kids Will Sit Still For 3: A Read-Aloud Guide*. Westport, CT: Libraries Unlimited.

Graduate School of Library and Information Science, University of Illinois at Urbana-Champaign. 2012. "Center for Children's Books." http://ccb .lis.illinois.edu.

Hennepin County Library. 2012. "Birth to Six." www.hclib.org/BirthTo6/.

Hillman, Judith. 2003. *Discovering Children's Literature*. Upper Saddle River, NJ: Merrill/Prentice Hall.

Kiefer, Barbara Z. 2010. *Charlotte Huck's Children's Literature*. New York: McGraw-Hill.

Lima, Carolyn W., and Rebecca L. Thomas. 2010. *A to Zoo: Subject Access to Children's Picture Books*. Westport, CT: Libraries Unlimited.

Lipson, Eden Ross. 2000. *The New York Times Parent's Guide to the Best Books for Children*. New York: Three Rivers Press.

Lukens, Rebecca. 2006. *A Critical Handbook of Children's Literature*. Boston: Allyn and Bacon.

Norton, Donna E., and Saundra E. Norton. 2010. *Through the Eyes of a Child: An Introduction to Children's Literature*. Upper Saddle River, NJ: Pearson Merrill/Prentice Hall.

Price, Anne, and Marguerita Rowland. 2010. *Children's Core Collection*. New York: H. W. Wilson.

Rowland, Marguerita, and Anne Price, eds. 2010. *Children's Catalog*. New York: H. W. Wilson.

School of Education, University of Wisconsin-Madison. 2012. "The Cooperative Children's Book Center (CCBC)." www.education.wisc.edu/ccbc/.

Short, Kathy G., Carol Lynch-Brown, and Carl M. Tomlinson. 2014. *Essentials of Children's Literature*. Boston: Pearson.

Source for Learning. 2012. "Read with Me! Books to Read with Your Child." www.teachersandfamilies.com/open/psreading.cfm.

Toussaint, Pamela. 1999. *Great Books for African-American Children*. New York: Plume.

Evaluation Tools

Cianciolo, Patricia J. 1997. *Picture Books for Children.* Chicago: American Library Association.

———. 2000. *Informational Picture Books for Children.* Chicago: American Library Association.

Darigan, Daniel L., Michael O. Tunnell, and James S. Jacobs. 2002. *Children's Literature: Engaging Teachers and Children in Good Books.* Upper Saddle River, NJ: Merrill/Prentice Hall.

England, Claire, and Adele M. Fasick. 1987. *ChildView: Evaluating and Reviewing Materials for Children.* Littleton, CO: Libraries Unlimited.

Giorgis, Cyndi, and Joan I. Glazer. 2013. *Literature for Young Children: Supporting Emergent Literacy, Ages 0–8.* Boston: Pearson.

Hearne, Betsy, and Roger Sutton, eds. 1993. *Evaluating Children's Books: A Critical Look: Aesthetic, Social, and Political Aspects of Analyzing and Using Children's Books.* Urbana-Champaign: University of Illinois, Graduate School of Library and Information Science.

Hillman, Judith. 2003. *Discovering Children's Literature.* Upper Saddle River, NJ: Merrill/Prentice Hall.

Horning, Kathleen T. 2010. *From Cover to Cover: Evaluating and Reviewing Children's Books.* New York: HarperCollins.

Kiefer, Barbara Z. 2010. *Charlotte Huck's Children's Literature.* New York: McGraw-Hill.

Lukens, Rebecca. 2003. *A Critical Handbook of Children's Literature.* Boston: Allyn and Bacon.

Lynch-Brown, Carol, and Carl M. Tomlinson. 2010. *Essentials of Children's Literature.* Boston: Allyn and Bacon.

Norton, Donna E., and Saundra E. Norton. 2010. *Through the Eyes of a Child: An Introduction to Children's Literature.* Upper Saddle River, NJ: Pearson Merrill/Prentice Hall.

Index of Authors, Illustrators, and Titles

CPSIA information can be obtained at www.ICGtesting.com
Printed in the USA
LVOW06s1258160815

450306LV00018B/922/P